River Cafe Cook Book Easy

Rose Gray and Ruth Rogers

EBURY
PRESS

Photography by Martyn Thompson   Design by the Senate

Frozen Sculpture by Marc Quinn

Contents

The Italian food in this book is easy to cook. Each recipe emphasises the things we value at the River Cafe – freshness, subtlety and quality – while being short, easy to shop for and easy to serve.

Simple, delicious food relies on its ingredients. Here you'll find a useful guide of what to keep in your store cupboard and in your fridge: olive oil, capers, balsamic vinegar, organic eggs, pancetta and more. Each recipe begins with a shopping list to make it easier to buy the things you'll need, and we've shown you where short-cuts can be taken.

We want you to feel inspired and confident in cooking Italian food. In chapters such as Tutti Ricotta we give many ways to use one basic ingredient. The pastas are divided into Spaghetti, Short Pasta and Tagliatelle to show how in Italian cooking each suggests a different type of sauce. You'll see that Gnocchi needn't be as hard to make as you think and that Carpaccio can mean beef or fish. Most of the recipes serve four and many are very quick to prepare, including a 15-minute Chocolate Cake.

Where we think it will be helpful we have added notes on ingredients, methods and equipment. There is a Sauces and Basics section at the end of the book which will provide you with the fundamentals of Italian cooking – like peeling tomatoes and preparing salted anchovies – and recipes for the sauces we use most. We have included a list of suppliers, though most of the ingredients are widely available.

Easy food doesn't have to mean unsophisticated food. Although the cook book concentrates on simplicity, there's always some surprise element, some little twist that comes from what we've learnt over the years, both at the River Cafe and when cooking with Italians in their kitchens. We hope you take as much pleasure in cooking these easy recipes as we do.

Rose Gray & Ruth Rogers, London 2003

1 Basic bruschetta

2 Asparagus Parmesan

3 Asparagus prosciutto

4 Tomato borlotti

5 Broccoli olives

6 Roast zucchini

7 Fennel olives

8 Fig rocket

9 Prosciutto spinach

10 Mozzarella olives

11 Mozzarella chillies

12 Borlotti prosciutto

13 Fennel prosciutto

14 Cavolo nero prosciutto

15 Tomato prosciutto

16 Chickpea chard

17 Ricotta red chillies

18 Tomato olives

19 Broad bean pecorino

20 Mozzarella anchovies

21 Crab lemon

22 Mozzarella tomato

23 Chickpea tomato

24 Grilled aubergine

Bruschetta

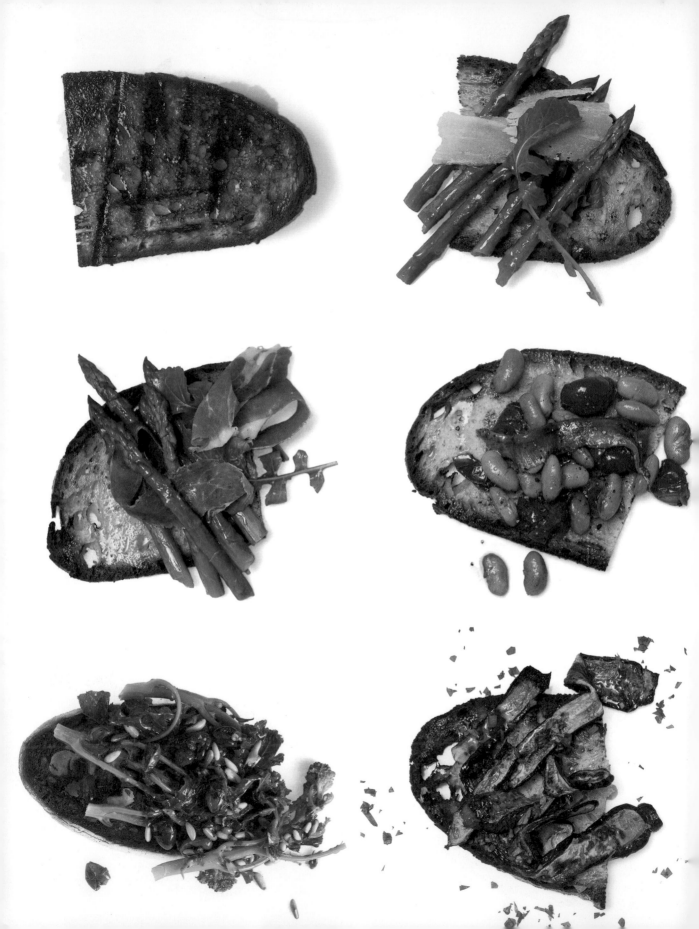

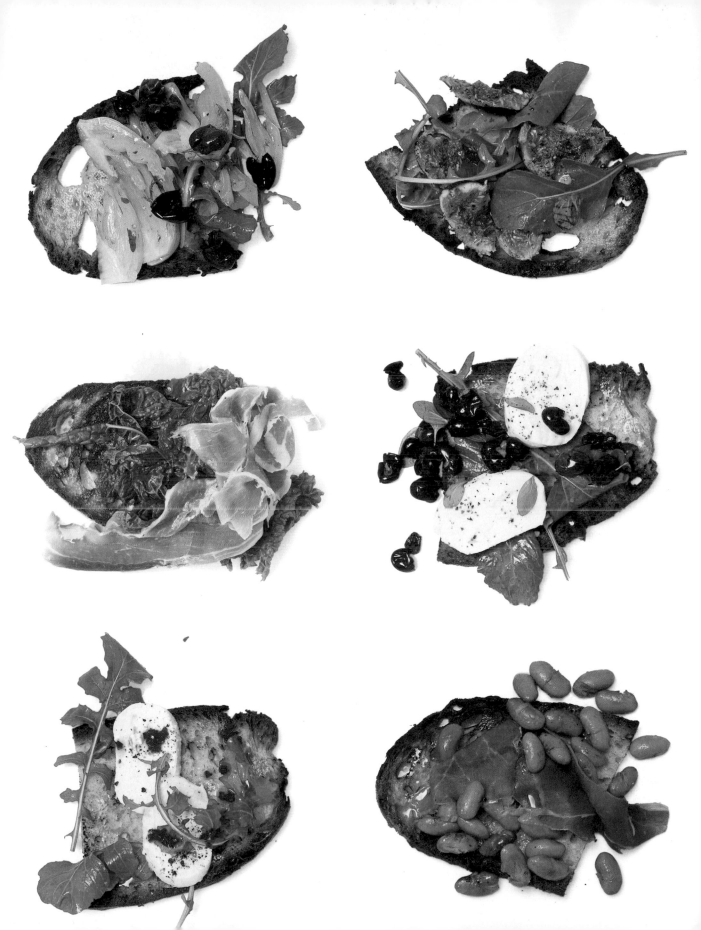

1 Basic bruschetta

Grill a generous piece of sourdough bread on both sides. Lightly rub one side with peeled garlic, season and pour over olive oil.

2 Asparagus Parmesan

Boil the asparagus until tender. While still warm, season and toss with olive oil and lemon. Add rocket, toss and then put on bruschetta with Parmesan shavings.

3 Asparagus prosciutto

Boil the asparagus until tender. While still warm, season and toss with olive oil and red wine vinegar. Add rocket, toss and then put on bruschetta with slices of prosciutto.

4 Tomato borlotti

Toss cherry tomatoes with olive oil and pieces of peeled garlic and season. Roast in a 200°C/Gas 6 oven for 15 minutes. Season warm borlotti beans and mix with olive oil and red wine vinegar. Combine with tomatoes. Place on bruschetta with an anchovy fillet.

5 Broccoli olives

Boil purple-sprouting broccoli until tender. Season and toss with olive oil and lemon. Put on bruschetta with stoned black olives and toasted pine nuts.

6 Roast zucchini

Cut zucchini lengthways into 5mm slices. Place on baking sheet, season, drizzle with olive oil and bake in a 200°C/Gas 6 oven until just crisp. Put on bruschetta with chopped fresh red chillies and mint, and drizzle with olive oil.

7 Fennel olives

Slice fennel bulb lengthways into 2cm pieces and boil until tender. Season and toss with olive oil and lemon. Add rocket and then put on bruschetta with chopped fresh red chillies and stoned black olives.

8 Fig rocket

Cut figs into quarters or eighths, depending on size. Season and toss with olive oil and balsamic vinegar. Add rocket, put on bruschetta and drizzle with olive oil.

9 Prosciutto spinach

Boil spinach until tender. Drain and press out the water. Season and toss with a generous amount of olive oil. Put on bruschetta with slices of prosciutto.

10 Mozzarella olives

Cut mozzarella into 1cm slices. Toss rocket with olive oil, lemon juice, and season. Put on bruschetta with stoned black olives, mozzarella, and marjoram. Sprinkle pepper over the mozzarella and drizzle with olive oil.

11 Mozzarella chillies

Cut mozzarella into 1cm slices. Toss rocket in olive oil, lemon juice, and season. Put on bruschetta with mozzarella, fresh red chillies and pepper. Drizzle with olive oil.

12 Borlotti prosciutto

Combine the warm borlotti beans with red wine vinegar, olive oil, and season. Place on bruschetta with slices of prosciutto. Drizzle with olive oil.

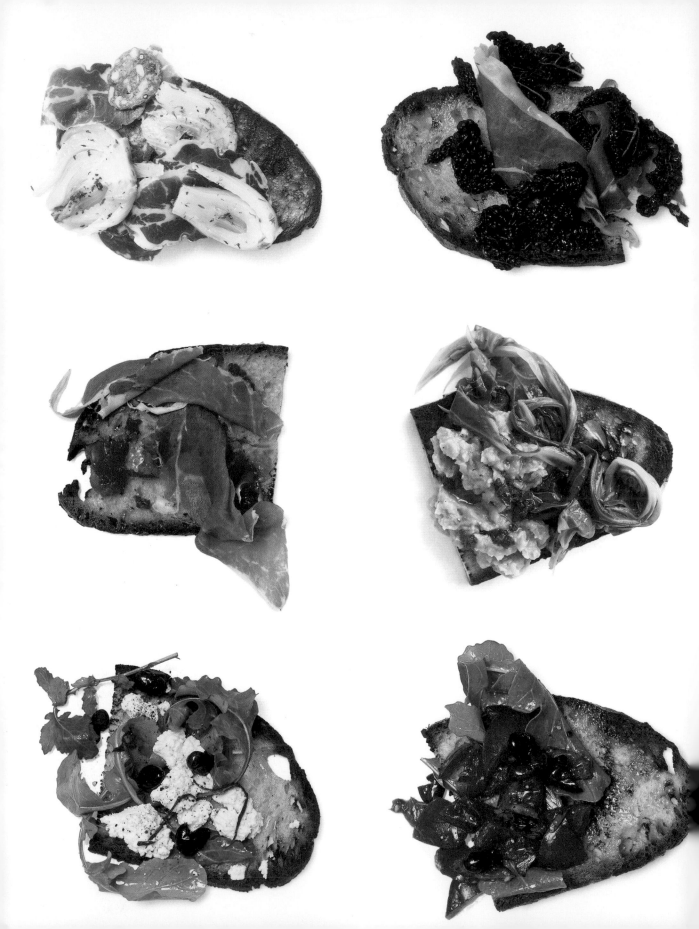

13 Fennel prosciutto

Slice the fennel lengthways into 1cm pieces. Reserve the leafy tops. Boil the pieces until tender. Toss while warm with olive oil, lemon juice, and season. Put on bruschetta with salami, prosciutto and scatter with the leafy fennel tops.

14 Cavolo nero prosciutto

Remove stalks from the tender leaves of cavolo nero and boil leaves until soft. Drain, season and toss with olive oil. Place on a bruschetta with slices of prosciutto. Serve while the cavolo is warm.

15 Tomato prosciutto

Cut a ripe large tomato in half and press the cut side on to bruschetta, squeezing the pulp and the juice into the bread. Rub with peeled garlic. Season and drizzle over olive oil. Serve with slices of prosciutto.

16 Chickpea chard

Boil the chard leaves until tender, drain well, and roughly chop. Braise in olive oil with garlic and season. Rinse chickpeas and briefly heat with olive oil and the juice of a lemon. Season and puree. Place puree and chard on a bruschetta. Spoon over chopped red chilli. Drizzle with olive oil.

17 Ricotta red chillies

Grill whole red chillies. Place in a bowl and cover with clingfilm. When cool, remove skins and seeds. Cover with olive oil. Toss rocket. Season with lemon juice and olive oil. Put on bruschetta with slices of ricotta, red chilli and stoned black olives.

18 Tomato olives

Cut plum tomatoes in half and squeeze out seeds and juices. Toss the flesh with olive oil, red wine vinegar and dried chilli. Season and then place on bruschetta with rocket and stoned black olives. Drizzle with olive oil.

19 Broad bean pecorino

Boil broad beans until tender. Drain and season, adding olive oil, lemon juice and fresh mint leaves. Put on bruschetta with shavings of fresh pecorino.

20 Mozzarella anchovies

Marinate rinsed salted anchovies in olive oil and lemon juice. Cut the mozzarella into 1cm slices. Toss rocket with olive oil and lemon juice and put on bruschetta with the anchovies. Season with black pepper and drizzle with olive oil.

21 Crab lemon

Mix white crab meat with lemon juice, olive oil, dried chilli, crushed fennel seeds and season. Toss salad leaves with lemon juice and olive oil and place with the crab on bruschetta. Drizzle with olive oil.

22 Mozzarella tomato

Toss together cherry tomatoes with olive oil and pieces of peeled garlic. Season and roast in a 200°C/Gas 6 oven for 15 minutes. Slice mozzarella into 1cm pieces. Toss rocket leaves with olive oil and lemon, place on bruschetta with tomatoes and slices of mozzarella. Drizzle with olive oil.

23 Chickpea tomato

Toss cherry tomatoes, olive oil, pieces of peeled garlic and rosemary. Season and roast in 200°C/Gas 6 oven for 15 minutes. Rinse the tinned chickpeas and heat with olive oil, dried chilli and season. Add to tomatoes. Rub bruschetta with rosemary and spoon over chickpeas and tomatoes. Drizzle with olive oil.

24 Grilled aubergine

Cut aubergines into very thin slices and grill on both sides. Toss with olive oil, lemon juice, and season. Add sliced basil and place on bruschetta with chopped fresh red chillies. Drizzle with olive oil.

Bruschetta

In its simplest form, bruschetta is grilled bread rubbed with garlic and drizzled with extra virgin olive oil. To make good bruschetta, you need bread that has a firm crumb, open texture, and a crisp crust. Where possible, choose a sourdough loaf, with a strong flavour which varies with the type of flour used.

The quality of the oil is equally important. The River Cafe bottles four single-estate cold-pressed Tuscan olive oils made from different varieties of olive, each with a distinctive character. We look for the freshest, greenest, most peppery oils. Pressed at the end of October, the oil is spiciest in the first few months, and more mellow later in the year, when it is also good for use in salads. Our olive oils are Selvapiana from Chianti Rufina, Morello from just north of Florence, Capezzana from Carmignano, and I Canonici from Polvereto (see suppliers' list, page 263).

1 Bread and tomato

2 Mozzarella and red pepper

3 Potato and parsley

4 Lentil and ricotta

5 Green bean and anchovy

6 Asparagus and anchovy

7 Porcini and Parmesan

8 Summer leaves

9 Mixed winter leaves

10 Puntarelle alla Romana

11 Crab and fennel salad

12 Toasted ciabatta salad

13 Roast beetroot

14 Raw fennel and Parmesan

15 Fresh borlotti bean salad

Antipasti

1

Bread and tomato

Plum tomatoes	6
Cherry tomatoes	10
Sourdough loaf	1/2
Red wine vinegar	2 tbs
Ex.v.olive oil	5 tbs
Basil leaves	4 tbs

Skin the plum tomatoes (see page 260), put in a food processor, and purée until smooth. Add the red wine vinegar and 2 tbs of the olive oil and season.

Crumble the stale bread in a bowl, add the puréed tomatoes and mix, using your hands, until totally combined.

Cut the cherry tomatoes in half, squeeze out the seeds and juice, season and add the flesh to the bread mixture with the basil.

Drizzle over the remaining olive oil.

Sourdough bread makes the best bruschetta and breadcrumbs. A loaf will last 3-4 days, and a stale one is best for breadcrumbs. If the bread is fresh, roughly tear it up and bake in a low oven to dry for 1/2 hour before crumbling.

2

Mozzarella and red pepper

Buffalo mozzarella	2
Red peppers	2
Cherry tomatoes	150g
Ex.v.olive oil	4 tbs
Plum tomatoes	4
Red wine vinegar	1 tbs
Basil leaves	4 tbs

Preheat the oven to 200°C/Gas 6, and preheat the grill or a griddle pan.

Toss the cherry tomatoes with 1 tbs of olive oil, season, and roast for 15 minutes.

Grill the peppers until black. Put in a plastic bag until cool then remove the skins, core and seeds. Tear lengthways into quarters. Slice the mozzarella.

Cut the plum tomatoes in half and squeeze out the seeds and juice. Cut each half in half.

Mix together the vinegar and remaining olive oil, season and pour over the tomatoes and pepper. Add the cherry tomatoes and the basil. Serve with the mozzarella.

3

Potato and parsley

Waxy potatoes	700g
Red wine vinegar	3 tbs
Ex.v.olive oil	4 tbs
Parsley leaves	3 tbs
Garlic clove	1

Peel and boil the potatoes in salted water until tender. Drain and while still warm slice 1cm thick. Carefully place on to a flat plate. Drizzle with the vinegar and olive oil, and season. Peel and chop the garlic and chop the parsley and scatter over the potatoes. Drizzle with more olive oil.

4

Lentil and ricotta

Lentils	175g
Ricotta	250g
Garlic clove	1
Ex.v.olive oil	
Red wine vinegar	1 tbs
Parsley leaves	2 tbs
Basil leaves	2 tbs
Rocket leaves	2 tbs

Wash the lentils. Put into a thick-bottomed pan with the peeled garlic and cover with water. Bring to the boil, and simmer for about 20 minutes. Drain, and remove the garlic. Add 3 tbs of olive oil and the vinegar. Season whilst still warm.

Chop the herbs and stir into the lentils to combine the flavours.

Turn the ricotta out carefully. Slice thinly and place over the lentils. Season and drizzle with olive oil.

Castelluccio (Italian) and Puy (French) lentils cook quickly, have distinctive nutty flavours and are equally delicious warm or cold.

5

Green bean and anchovy

Green beans	500g
Anchovy fillets	10
Ex.v.olive oil	
Capers	25g
Lemon	1
Basil leaves	2 tbs
Niçoise olives	100g

Boil the beans in salted water until soft. Drain, then season and toss with 2 tbs of olive oil.

Chop the rinsed anchovies and capers together, put into a bowl, and stir in lemon juice to combine. Add 2 tbs olive oil and stir.

Stone the olives and tear the basil. Mix the beans into the sauce. Scatter over olives and basil.

Anchovies preserved in salt and then rinsed, will 'melt' much more effectively than anchovies preserved in oil, as the oil acts as a barrier (see page 260).

6

Asparagus and anchovy

Asparagus	800g
Anchovy fillets	6
Unsalted butter	150g
Lemon	1/2
Ex.v.olive oil	
Parmesan	50g

Soften the butter. Rinse, dry and roughly chop the anchovies.

In a bowl mix the anchovies with lemon juice and black pepper then with a fork mix with the butter.

Boil the asparagus in salted water until tender. Drain and season and drizzle with olive oil.

Place the asparagus on warm plates. Spoon over the anchovy butter, and scatter with Parmesan shavings.

Choose asparagus with tightly closed tips and firm stalks. Asparagus steamers are designed to protect the fragile tips as they cook standing upright. Alternatively, lay the asparagus flat in a large frying pan and cover with boiling salted water.

Porcini and Parmesan

Fresh porcini	400g
Parmesan	50g
Parsley leaves	2 tbs
Dried chilli	1
Lemon	1
Ex.v.olive oil	

Cut thin slices of the porcini lengthways through the stem. Finely chop the parsley and crumble the chilli.

Mix the parsley with the juice of 1/2 lemon and 2 tbs of olive oil. Season.

Place the porcini slices over each plate. Scatter with chilli, and season. Squeeze over the remainder of the lemon juice. Scatter the parsley and cover with Parmesan shavings. Drizzle with olive oil.

Look for medium-sized, firm fresh porcini for this salad, and trim away the earthy bits at the base. Peel the stem but do not detach from the cap. Wipe the caps with a damp cloth.

8

Summer leaves

Mixed leaves	250g
Pecorino staginata	200g
Black olives	2 tbs
Marjoram leaves	2 tbs
Garlic clove	1
Red wine vinegar	1 tbs
Ex.v.olive oil	3 tbs
Lemon	1/2

Wash the leaves and spin dry. Stone the olives, chop the marjoram, peel and chop the garlic, and mix these in a bowl with the vinegar and 2 tbs olive oil. Season.

Stir together the lemon juice and remaining olive oil and season. Pour over the leaves and toss. Spoon over the olives and cover with pecorino shavings.

Summer leaf salad could include the cucumber-flavoured purslane, available in Greek, Turkish and Lebanese shops, nasturtium leaves, the small leaves from fresh beetroots, spinach, sorrel and Swiss chard. Orache is an unusual Mediterranean plant with a metallic flavour – pick the small red leaves before the plant flowers. Certain edible flowers are also delicious: white cultivated rocket flowers are peppery, while zucchini flowers add colour. Fresh summer herbs such as basil, mint and marjoram, used sparingly are an interesting addition. Pecorino staginata is the hard, aged Tuscan pecorino.

9   Mixed winter leaves

Mixed leaves	250g	Wash the leaves and spin dry.
Balsamic vinegar	2 tbs	
Ex.v.olive oil	5 tbs	Stir together the vinegar and olive oil and season. Pour over the leaves, and toss to coat each leaf.

To make a winter salad interesting use bitter leaves such as cultivated dandelion, cicoria, gremolo verde, trevise, radicchio, and red and white chicory. Lemony sorrel, peppery rocket, hot mustard leaf, metallic spinach and fresh lamb's lettuce are in season too. You could also include winter herbs such as mint, flat-leaf parsley, the pale yellow centre leaves of celery, and the green tips of Florence fennel.

10

Puntarelle alla Romana

Puntarelle heads	2
Salted anchovies	5
Red wine vinegar	2 tbs
Garlic clove	1
Dried chillies	2
Black pepper	1 tsp
Ex.v.olive oil	
Lemon	1

To prepare puntarelle, fill a bowl with cold water and ice cubes. Pull the hollow buds from the puntarelle heads. Using a small knife, slice the buds very thinly lengthways. Place in the water to crisp and curl up. This will take an hour.

Rinse and fillet the anchovies (see page 260), cut into 1cm pieces, and place in a small bowl. Cover with the vinegar, and stir to allow the anchovy to dissolve. Peel and chop the garlic very finely and add to the anchovies with the crumbled chilli and pepper. Leave for 15 minutes, and then add 4 tbs olive oil.

Spin-dry the puntarelle as for salad. Place in a bowl and spoon over the anchovy sauce. Serve with lemon.

This unusual salad is traditionally Roman. Puntarelle now comes into the New Covent Garden market, which supplies specialist greengrocers and Italian restaurants. The season starts in November and ends in February (see suppliers' list, page 263).

11

Crab and fennel salad

Crab cooked in shell	2kg
Fennel bulbs	2
Ex.v.olive oil	
Lemons	1½
Dried chilli	1
Parsley leaves	1 tbs

For the fennel salad, cut off the leafy tops. Cut the fennel across into 5mm slices to make rings. Preheat the grill and grill the fennel on both sides, until lightly charred. Season and toss with 2 tbs olive oil and the juice of ½ lemon.

Crumble the chilli and finely chop the parsley and fennel tops.

For the crab, pick the white and brown meat out of the shell, keeping them separate. Stir the chilli, parsley and fennel tops into the white meat. Season and add 1 tbs lemon juice and 2 tbs of olive oil.

Season the brown meat. Serve the crab meats with the fennel salad, drizzle with olive oil and serve with lemon.

For crab salad you need freshly picked crab. Choose a cooked crab that smells fresh and has its legs drawn up into the body. This indicates the crab was alive when cooked and will taste sweet and delicious. Picking crab does take time and is a task best shared.

12

Toasted ciabatta salad

Ciabatta loaf	1
Tomatoes	500g
Capers	50g
Garlic clove	1
Red wine vinegar	2 tbs
Ex.v.olive oil	
Anchovy fillets	8
Basil leaves	3 tbs

Preheat the oven to 200°C/Gas 6.

Skin the tomatoes (see page 260) and cut each in half. Over a sieve, spoon out the fleshy insides and push as much of the juice through as you can. Put the tomato halves in a bowl with the rinsed capers and season.

Crush the peeled garlic with 1 tsp salt. Stir into the juice. Add the vinegar, 5 tbs of the olive oil, and season.

Trim the crust off the base of the bread. Tear into thin leaf-like pieces, season and place in an oven tray. Drizzle with olive oil and bake in the oven until light brown and crunchy. Put the hot bread pieces in a large bowl. Pour over the juice and add a little more olive oil. Mix in the tomatoes, and add the anchovies and basil. Serve warm.

Mix a variety of tomatoes such as yellow marigold, fleshy oxheart and cherry vine to make this salad more unusual.

13

Roast beetroot

Beetroots	14
Garlic cloves	2
Thyme leaves	2 tbs
Ex.v.olive oil	
Rocket leaves	100g
Red wine vinegar	3 tbs
Horseradish stick	1/4

Preheat the oven to 200°C/Gas 6.

Cut the peeled garlic in half. Cut the leaves 2cm from the beetroot (keep to use in a salad). Scrub the beetroots thoroughly, then place in an oven tray. Season generously, scatter with thyme and garlic, and drizzle with olive oil.

Cover loosely with foil and bake in the oven for 20 minutes. Remove the foil, turn the beetroots round in the olive oil, and continue roasting for a further 1/2 hour.

Cut the beetroots in half and arrange on plates. Place the rocket amongst them. Season, and drizzle with 4 tbs olive oil and vinegar. Grate over the fresh horseradish.

Buy beetroots sold with their leaves attached, root tail intact, and golf-ball sized. Look for different varieties. Golden are a rich deep yellow and very sweet. There is also a striped variety and a long, oval variety that is deep red and has a strong beet flavour. Horseradish has always been grown in traditional vegetable gardens and allotments, and also grows wild in many places. The plant is cultivated for the root, which needs to be peeled before being grated on the finest part of the grater.

14

Raw fennel and Parmesan

Fennel bulbs	3
Parmesan	50g
Lemon juice	3 tbs
Ex.v.olive oil	4 tbs
Prosciutto slices	12

Trim the fennel. Chop the leafy tops.

Slice the bulbs lengthways very thinly and toss together with the lemon juice and olive oil, then season. Shave the Parmesan and combine. Leave to marinate for 1 hour, tossing occasionally. Before serving, add the fennel tops. Serve with prosciutto or salami.

15

Fresh borlotti bean salad

Fresh borlotti beans	1kg
Garlic cloves	2
Sage leaves	3 tbs
Red wine vinegar	1 tbs
French mustard	2 tbs
Ex.v.olive oil	5 tbs
Rocket leaves	250g

Pod the beans and cover with cold water. Add the peeled garlic and sage leaves. Bring to the boil, and simmer for 35 minutes until soft. Drain and season.

Combine the vinegar and mustard, and season. Slowly add the olive oil.

Toss the beans with two-thirds of the dressing. Toss the leaves in the remainder of the dressing.

Divide the dressed leaves between the plates. Spoon the beans over the leaves, and serve with the bean juices over.

Fresh borlotti have magenta and white pods and beans. The season for borlotti is summer (see suppliers' list, page 263).

1 Beef carpaccio

2 Sea bass carpaccio

3 Tuna carpaccio

4 Marinated anchovies

5 Beef fillet with thyme

Carpaccio

1

Beef carpaccio

Beef fillet	500g
Ex.v.olive oil	350ml
Pine nuts	50g
Parmesan	100g
Lemons	2

Cut the fillet at a slight angle into 2mm slices. Lay each slice on clingfilm, and cover with another piece of clingfilm. Beat flat to extend and thin out each slice.

Pour in olive oil to cover the bottom of a dish that will hold the beef slices in 2 layers. Season the fillet generously on both sides, and arrange a layer in the dish. Pour over more olive oil and repeat with another layer. The slices should be submerged. Cover with clingfilm and place in the fridge for 1/2 hour.

Lightly toast the pine nuts over a gentle heat in a dry frying pan. Shave the Parmesan into slithers.

To serve, lift the beef slices from the marinade and put on a plate. Scatter with the pine nuts and the Parmesan. Serve with lemon.

This unusual version of carpaccio comes from Verona and is often served with Grilled radicchio (see page 210). Ask for short fillet, the fine-grained centre cut, otherwise known as the chateaubriand.

2

Sea bass carpaccio

Sea bass	2.5kg
Cherry tomatoes	8
Lemons	2
Dried chillies	3
Ex.v.olive oil	3 tbs
Marjoram leaves	3 tbs

Place the bass fillets skin side down on a board. Using a long-bladed knife, cut the slices as finely as you can along the whole length of the fillet. Place the slices side by side on cold plates.

Squeeze the juices and a little pulp out of the tomatoes over the bass. The tomato acids will slightly 'cook' the fish. Drizzle with lemon juice, season and add a few flakes of chilli. Finally pour over 3 tbs olive oil and scatter with a few marjoram leaves. Serve with lemon.

Ask the fishmonger to clean, scale and cut the fish into 2 fillets. The fillet cut from a large sea bass weighing around 2.5kg is the easiest to finely slice. Sea bass for carpaccio should always be very fresh. Medium to large line-caught wild fish will always have the best flavour.

3

Tuna carpaccio

Tuna loin	500g
Capers	30g
Lemons	3
Ex.v.olive oil	
Rocket leaves	100g

To make the slicing easier, wrap the piece of tuna tightly in clingfilm and place in the freezer for 2 hours to firm up.

Marinate the rinsed capers for $1/2$ hour in the juice of $1/2$ lemon, and enough olive oil to cover.

Use a long-bladed knife to cut the tuna across the grain as thinly as you possibly can.

Arrange the slices on cold plates, and season. Scatter over the capers and the rocket, and drizzle with the juice of a whole lemon and olive oil. Serve with lemon.

Small spiky-leafed wild rocket, known as Capri rocket or Turkish rocket, is best for this recipe, as its hot, peppery taste contrasts with the oily richness of the tuna. Salted capers have a fresher taste than those preserved in vinegar. Wash off the salt before marinating.

4

Marinated anchovies

Fresh anchovies	500g
Rosemary sprig	1
Fennel seeds	1 tsp
Dried chilli	1
Lemons	2
Ex.v.olive oil	
Red wine vinegar	3 tbs

To fillet the anchovies, pull the head and spine away from the fish, then pull off the tails and fins to make two fillets. Rinse and lay out on kitchen paper.

Chop the rosemary finely and mix immediately with 1 tbs salt. Grind the fennel seeds, and crumble the chilli.

Scatter some of the rosemary, fennel, chilli and black pepper over the surface of a serving dish. Drizzle with lemon juice and olive oil.

Place the anchovies skin side up in the dish, packing them closely together. Sprinkle them with rosemary, fennel, chilli, black pepper, lemon, vinegar and olive oil. Make further layers, repeating the process.

Make sure the final layer is submerged.

Cover with clingfilm and leave to 'cook' in the marinade for at least an hour.

Fresh anchovies marinated in this way will keep for up to 2 days in a fridge. They are delicious served with bruschetta and a mixed-leaf salad.

5

Beef fillet with thyme

Beef fillet	500g
Black peppercorns	30g
Thyme leaves	3 tbs
Ex.v.olive oil	
Lemons	3
Parmesan	100g
Wild rocket leaves	100g

Grind the peppercorns and mix with $1/2$ tbs of salt and the thyme.

Rub the fillet lightly with olive oil, then rub the pepper mixture into the beef. Heat a ridged griddle pan to very hot, and sear the beef on all sides. Cool.

Use a long, sharp-bladed knife to slice the beef as thinly as possible. Place the slices on a board and press with the flat blade of the knife to extend each slice.

Cover a cold plate with the beef. Season, and drizzle over the juice of $1/2$ lemon.

Shave the Parmesan. Toss the rocket with olive oil and a little more lemon juice. Scatter the leaves over the beef, then put the Parmesan shavings on top. Drizzle over more olive oil, and serve with lemon.

1 Broad bean

2 Pappa pomodoro

3 Cavolo nero

4 Pea, pancetta and zucchini

5 Artichoke and potato

6 Rice and potato

7 Clam and fennel

8 Zucchini and cannellini

9 Pumpkin crostini

10 Quick fish

11 Chickpea and shrimp

Soup

1

Broad bean

Podded broad beans	300g
Podded peas	200g
Garlic cloves	2
Waxy potatoes	400g
Basil leaves	4 tbs
Ex.v.olive oil	
Chicken stock	300ml
Sourdough loaf	1/4

Peel and chop the garlic. Peel and cut the potatoes into 2cm cubes.

Heat 2 tbs of olive oil in a thick-bottomed pan and fry the garlic until soft. Add the potato, stir and season, then add the broad beans, peas and stock. Cook for 15 minutes until the potatoes are soft. Place half the soup in a food processor and roughly pulse, then return to the same pan. Add the basil. The soup should be thick.

Preheat the oven to 200ºC/Gas 6. Thickly slice the bread, trim the crusts and tear into pieces. Drizzle with olive oil. Season and bake until lightly toasted.

Put the bread in the bowls. Spoon the soup over and drizzle with olive oil.

This very thick soup of broad beans and potatoes requires very little stock, as the flavour is in the beans and basil. It is fine to use a quality ready-made chicken stock in this recipe.

2

Pappa pomodoro

Tin tomatoes	2 x 400g
Garlic cloves	2
Sourdough loaf	1/4
Chicken stock	200ml
Ex.v.olive oil	
Sage leaves	2 tbs

Peel and slice the garlic. Slice the bread into 1cm slices.

Heat a thick-bottomed pan. Add the stock and 6 tbs of olive oil, the sage and the garlic. When the stock begins to evaporate and the garlic starts to colour, add the bread. Fry over a high heat until the stock is absorbed and the bread is crisp.

Add the tomatoes and season. Stir to break up the bread and cook for 15 minutes. Pour over enough water to loosen the soup. It should be a thick consistency. Cook for a further 5 minutes.

Serve with more olive oil.

The flavour of this thick soup comes from frying the bread in the stock and olive oil before adding the tomatoes. It is fine to use a quality ready-made chicken stock. In the summer make the soup with 500g of skinned and seeded fresh tomatoes.

3

Cavolo nero

Cavolo nero	500g
Garlic cloves	4
Red onions	2
Carrots	4
Celery head	1
Dried chilli	1
Tin borlotti beans	400g
Ex.v.olive oil	
Fennel seeds	½ tsp
Tin tomatoes	1 x 200g
Chicken stock	500ml
Sourdough loaf	¼

Peel the garlic, onion and carrots. Roughly chop 3 garlic cloves, the onion, pale celery heart and carrots. Crumble the chilli. Drain and rinse the beans.

Heat 3 tbs of olive oil in a thick-bottomed pan, add the onion, celery and carrot and cook gently until soft. Add the fennel seed, chilli and garlic and stir, then add the tomatoes, chopping them as they cook. Season, and simmer for 15 minutes, stirring occasionally. Add the beans and stock, and cook for another 15 minutes.

Discard the stalks from the cavolo nero and boil the leaves in salted water for 5 minutes, drain and chop. Keep 4 tbs of the water. Add the water and cavolo to the soup. Stir and season.

Cut the bread into 1.5cm slices. Toast on both sides, then rub with the remaining garlic and drizzle with olive oil. Break up the toast and divide between the soup bowls. Spoon over the soup and serve with more olive oil.

All bean soups are made more delicious with a generous addition of the spicy-flavoured newly pressed olive oil poured over each serving. Tuscan olive oil is pressed at the end of October, which is also when the frosty weather starts and cavolo nero is ready to be picked.

4

Pea, pancetta and zucchini

Podded peas	500g
Pancetta slices	4
Zucchini	1kg
Garlic cloves	2
Red onion	1
Mint leaves	3 tbs
Ex.v.olive oil	
Chicken stock	250ml
Double cream	150ml

Cut the zucchini into small pieces. Peel and chop the garlic and onion, and cut the pancetta into matchsticks. Chop the mint.

In a thick-bottomed pan heat 2 tbs of the olive oil and gently fry the onion with the pancetta. Cook until soft, then add the garlic and zucchini. Stir and cook for 15 minutes. Add 2 tbs of water to loosen.

Boil the peas in salted water, drain and add to the zucchini. Add the stock and bring to the boil. Cook for a further 5 minutes.

Pulse chop in a food processor. Return to the pan, add the chopped mint and cream, and stir. Season and serve at room temperature.

5 Artichoke and potato

Artichokes	6 small
Potatoes	200g
Garlic cloves	3
Dried chilli	1
Parsley leaves	4 tbs
Ex.v.olive oil	
Chicken stock	500ml
Ciabatta loaf	1

To prepare the artichokes, break off the outer leaves until you get to the tender heart. Cut off the tips and peel the stalks. Cut into eighths and remove any choke.

Peel the potatoes and cut into pieces the same size as the artichokes. Peel and chop the garlic. Crumble the chilli and chop the parsley.

Heat 3 tbs of olive oil in a thick-bottomed pan. Lightly brown the artichokes, add the garlic, dried chilli and 1 tbs of the parsley. Add half the stock, 200ml of water, season and cover. Simmer for 15 minutes.

Add the potatoes and the rest of the stock – there should be just enough to cover the soup. Cook until the potatoes are soft.

Cut ciabatta into 1cm slices, toast on both sides, rub with garlic, drizzle with olive oil.

Mash the soup – which should be thick – to a rough consistency. Stir in the remaining parsley and pour over olive oil. Serve with a crostini.

Preparing artichokes is easier if you use a 'Y' shaped potato peeler for trimming the hearts and stems and a melon baller for removing the chokes.

6

Rice and potato

Risotto rice	200g
Potatoes	500g
Red onion	1
Carrots	2
Celery	2
Parsley leaves	3 tbs
Pecorino	100g
Ex.v.olive oil	3 tbs
Chicken stock	500ml
Bay leaves	2

Peel the potatoes, and cut into 5mm cubes. Peel and finely chop the onion, carrots and celery. Chop the parsley and grate the pecorino.

In a thick-bottomed pan heat the olive oil, add the onion, carrot and celery, and cook until soft. Add the potato and cook for 5 minutes until lightly coloured. Stir in half the stock and the bay. Stir and scrape up the vegetables, and simmer for 20 minutes.

Add the rice and the remaining stock, season and cook, stirring, for a further 20 minutes until the rice is tender. Add more stock if the soup is too thick.

Stir the parsley into the soup and serve with pecorino.

This soup has very subtle flavours, so it is worth the effort of making your own chicken stock.

7

Clam and fennel

Clams	1.5kg
Fennel bulbs	2
Parsley leaves	3 tbs
Dried chillies	2
Garlic cloves	4
Ex.v.olive oil	
White wine	200ml
Ciabatta loaf	1
Lemon	1

Clean the clams. Finely slice the fennel, keeping the leafy tops, chop the parsley, crumble the chilli, and peel and finely chop 3 of the garlic cloves.

Boil the fennel in salted water until tender. Drain.

Heat 2 tbs olive oil in a thick-bottomed pan, add the garlic and chilli, and cook until soft. Add the clams, fennel and wine. Cover and cook until the clams open, a few minutes. Discard any that remain closed. Add the parsley and the fennel tops, and season.

Cut the bread into 1.5cm slices. Toast, rub with the remaining garlic clove and put into warm bowls. Pour the clams, fennel and juices over. Drizzle with olive oil and serve with lemon.

8

Zucchini and cannellini

Zucchini	500g
Tin cannellini beans	400g
Celery head	1
Garlic clove	1
Parsley leaves	3 tbs
Ex.v.olive oil	

Finely chop the pale celery heart. Cut the zucchini into halves lengthways and roughly cut them to make small pieces. Peel and finely chop the garlic and chop the parsley. Drain and rinse the beans.

Heat 1 tbs olive oil in a thick-bottomed pan and fry the celery and parsley until soft. Add the garlic and zucchini and fry for 10 minutes. Add 5 tbs of water and scrape up to combine. Add the beans. Stir and cook for a further 5 minutes. Mash roughly and drizzle with olive oil.

Fresh cannellini beans sold in their pods are absolutely delicious and can be found in shops throughout July and August. Dried cannellini beans are good too, but you have to plan ahead, as the beans need to be soaked for at least 12 hours before cooking (see page 261). Tinned cannellini beans, washed thoroughly, can also be used for this recipe.

9

Pumpkin crostini

Pumpkin	500g
Pancetta	100g
Garlic cloves	2
Red onions	2
Fennel bulb	1
Dried chilli	1
Fennel seeds	1 tbs
Ex.v.olive oil	
Tin tomatoes	1 x 200g
Sourdough loaf	1/4

Peel and cut the pumpkin into 2cm cubes. Cut the pancetta into matchsticks. Peel and chop 1 garlic clove, the onions and the parsley and slice and chop the fennel. Crumble the chilli and grind the fennel seeds.

In a thick-bottomed pan heat 2 tbs olive oil and gently fry the pancetta, then add the onion, fennel, garlic, chilli and fennel seeds. Season and cook for 5 minutes. Add the pumpkin and stir to combine. Add the tomatoes, breaking them up, and season. Cover and simmer for 15 minutes or until the vegetables are soft.

Cut the bread into 1cm slices. Toast on both sides, rub with the remaining peeled garlic clove, and put in the bowls. Spoon the soup over and drizzle with olive oil.

Onion squash, with its bright orange flesh and slightly dry, potato-like texture, is the best pumpkin for this soup.

10

Quick fish

Langoustines	4-8
Clams	300g
Red mullet fillet	350g
Potatoes	350g
Garlic cloves	2
Dried chillies	2
Parsley leaves	2 tbs
Fresh root ginger	50g
Lemon	1
Ex.v.olive oil	
Tin chopped tomatoes	400g
White wine	150ml

Peel the potatoes and the garlic. Quarter the potatoes, slice the garlic, crumble the chilli and chop the parsley. Grate the ginger and squeeze the lemon.

Heat 2 tbs olive oil in a thick-bottomed pan. Add the potatoes, garlic and chilli, and cook to colour.

Add the tomatoes to the potatoes and season. Cook for 15 minutes or until the potatoes are soft.

Stir in the ginger. Add all the fish, and then pour over the lemon juice and the wine. Season and cover. Simmer for 5 minutes. The clams should be open and the langoustines firm.

Add the parsley and serve with olive oil drizzled over.

Ask the fishmonger to fillet the mullet. To serve 4, you will need 8 small or 4 large langoustines.

11

Chickpea and shrimp

Tin chickpeas	400g
Peeled shrimps	400g
Dried porcini	30g
Tin chopped tomatoes	400g
Garlic cloves	3
Dried chillies	2
Ex.v.olive oil	
Dried oregano	2 tbs
Lemon	1/2
Ciabatta loaf	1

Soak the porcini in 200ml hot water. Drain and rinse the chickpeas. Peel and chop 2 garlic cloves, and crumble the chilli.

Strain the porcini, keeping the liquid, and roughly chop.

Heat a thick-bottomed pan with 2 tbs of olive oil, and add half the chopped garlic, the porcini, oregano, chilli, and season. Cook for 4 minutes. Add the tomatoes, and simmer for 20 minutes, adding a little of the porcini water as the tomatoes reduce, to keep the soup liquid.

In a separate pan heat 1 tbs of olive oil and add the remaining chopped garlic. When coloured, add the shrimps and chickpeas, and stir to warm through. Season. Add the juice of the 1/2 lemon. Mix together with the tomato.

Cut the bread into slices. Toast on both sides, rub with remaining peeled garlic clove, and put in bowls. Pour the soup over and drizzle with olive oil.

1 Sardinian bottarga

2 Butter and cheese

3 Marinated raw tomato

4 Garlic, chilli and parsley

5 Pea and spring onions

6 Tomato and anchovy

7 Clam and Prosecco

8 Zucchini and capers

9 Spaghetti in a bag

Spaghetti

1

Sardinian bottarga

Spaghetti	320g
Bottarga	200g
Lemons	3
Dried chillies	2
Ex.v.olive oil	100ml

Squeeze the juice of 2 of the lemons. Crumble the chillies.

Grate 3/4 of the bottarga into a bowl. Add the lemon juice and stir to combine to a cream. Slowly add the olive oil to form a thick sauce.

Cook the spaghetti in boiling salted water until al dente. Drain and reserve a little of the cooking water.

Stir the hot water into the bottarga cream to loosen, then season with chilli and black pepper. Add the spaghetti to the sauce and toss to coat thoroughly.

Serve with the remaining bottarga grated over, and a piece of lemon.

In this recipe, use bottarga di mugine, which is the sun-dried, salted roe of the grey mullet (see suppliers' list, page 263).

2

Butter and cheese

Spaghetti	320g
Unsalted butter	100g
Pecorino Romano	50g
Parmesan	50g

Cook the spaghetti in boiling salted water until al dente. Grate the cheeses whilst the pasta is cooking. Drain, reserving 4 tbs of the water.

Put the reserved water and the butter back into the hot pan and simmer very gently over a low heat. Stir until the butter melts into the water. Remove from the heat and stir in half the pecorino and Parmesan. Add the spaghetti and toss to coat thoroughly. Serve with more Parmesan and pecorino.

This simple combination of pecorino and Parmesan is found in many Roman trattorias where it is called 'cacio e pepe'. Made with sheep's milk, pecorino from different regions in Italy varies greatly in flavour and texture. Pecorino Romano, used mostly in cooking, is a hard, strong flavoured aged cheese found in the south of Italy.

3

Marinated raw tomato

Spaghetti	320g
Cherry tomatoes	600g
Basil leaves	3 tbs
Ex.v.olive oil	
Red wine vinegar	2 tbs
Balsamic vinegar	1 tbs

Cut the tomatoes in half and squeeze to remove juice and seeds. Tear the basil.

In a bowl combine 6 tbs of the olive oil and the vinegars, and season. Add the tomato halves, slightly pressing the tomatoes down to absorb the flavour of the vinegar and olive oil. Add the basil, stir, cover and leave to marinate for an hour. Do not refrigerate.

Cook the spaghetti in boiling salted water until al dente. Drain and return to the pan. Add the tomatoes over a high heat. Stir to combine. Drizzle with olive oil.

4

Garlic, chilli and parsley

Spaghetti	320g
Garlic cloves	6
Dried chillies	3
Parsley	10 tbs
Ex.v.olive oil	120ml
Lemon	1/2

Peel and cut the garlic into slices. Chop the parsley and crumble the chillies. In a thick-bottomed pan heat the olive oil and gently fry the garlic until soft but not brown. Add the chillies, squeeze over lemon juice. Remove from heat, then stir in the parsley. Season.

Cook the spaghetti in boiling salted water until al dente. Drain and stir in the garlic sauce. Drizzle with olive oil.

5

Pea and spring onions

Spaghetti	320g
Podded peas	400g
Spring onions	100g
Garlic clove	1
Prosciutto	100g
Parsley leaves	2 tbs
Parmesan	50g
Unsalted butter	100g
Ex.v.olive oil	

Roughly chop the white part of the onions. Peel and finely chop the garlic and tear the prosciutto into pieces. Chop the parsley. Grate the Parmesan.

Melt the butter in a large frying pan. Add the onions and gently soften, then add the peas, salt and 3 tbs of hot water. Simmer gently until the water evaporates.

Add the garlic and parsley to the peas plus 3 tbs of olive oil. Cover and cook over low heat for 15 minutes. Add the prosciutto. If more liquid is needed, add olive oil, not water. When the peas are soft and a dark green colour, remove from heat.

Cook the spaghetti in boiling salted water until al dente, then drain. Add to the peas, and serve with Parmesan.

Tomato and anchovy

Spaghetti	320g
Cherry tomatoes	500g
Lemon	1
Anchovy fillets	10
Garlic cloves	2
Dried chillies	2
Basil leaves	3 tbs
Ex.v.olive oil	

Cut the tomatoes in half and squeeze out seeds and juice. Squeeze the lemon.

Peel and finely chop the garlic, crumble the chilli, and rinse the anchovies. Tear the basil leaves.

Heat 3 tbs of the olive oil in a thick-bottomed pan, add the garlic and chilli, and fry for a minute, then add the anchovies and 3 tbs of water. Add the tomatoes, lemon juice, and season. Raise the heat, cook for 2-3 minutes, stirring to combine. Remove from the heat and add the basil.

Cook the spaghetti in boiling salted water until al dente, drain and add to the sauce. Toss to coat the spaghetti thoroughly. Serve with olive oil drizzled over.

7

Clam and Prosecco

Spaghetti	320g
Small clams	3kg
Prosecco	250ml
Garlic cloves	3
Parsley leaves	2 tbs
Dried chillies	2
Ex.v.olive oil	3 tbs
Lemons	2

Wash the clams. Peel and finely chop the garlic, chop the parsley, and crumble the chilli.

Heat the olive oil in a thick-bottomed pan. Add the garlic and cook until just coloured. Add the chilli, the clams and Prosecco, cover and cook over a high heat to open the clams, about 3 minutes. Discard any clams that do not open. Season and keep warm.

Cook the spaghetti in boiling salted water until al dente, drain and add to the clam sauce. Cook together over high heat for 2 minutes, tossing thoroughly. Remove any empty shells. Serve with the parsley and lemon.

8

Zucchini and capers

Spaghetti	320g
Zucchini	400g
Garlic cloves	2
Dried chillies	2
Sea salt	1 tbs
Capers	3 tbs
Tomatoes	250g
Dried oregano	2 tsp
Ex.v.olive oil	
White wine vinegar	2 tbs
Oregano leaves	2 tsp

Cut the zucchini (see note below), peel and chop the garlic and crumble the chillies. Rinse the capers. Place the zucchini in a colander, scatter with the sea salt, and leave for 15 minutes. Squeeze and pat dry.

Cut the tomatoes in half or quarters if large. Squeeze out the juice and seeds, reserving the juice. Combine the tomato pieces with the juice then add the capers, chilli, dried oregano and garlic. Stir in 3 tbs of the olive oil and the vinegar and season. Leave to marinate for 15 minutes.

Heat 2 tbs olive oil in a thick-bottomed frying pan. When hot, add the zucchini and fry to lightly brown. Season. Stir in the tomatoes and remove from the heat.

Cook the spaghetti in boiling salted water until al dente, drain. Add to the sauce, turn to coat each strand, then mix in the fresh oregano and drizzle with olive oil.

If your zucchini are large, 15cm or bigger, try this method for cutting them into matchsticks: slice the zucchini into 5mm discs then cut each disc into 5mm width strips.

9

Spaghetti in a bag

Spaghetti	320g
Tomato sauce	4 tbs
Ex.v.olive oil	
Garlic cloves	2
Fresh red chilli	1
Peeled prawns	500g
Basil leaves	2 tbs
White wine	120ml
Lemons	2

Preheat the oven to 200ºC/Gas 6. Make the Tomato sauce (see page 259).

Cook the spaghetti in boiling salted water for only 7 minutes, then drain. Put in a bowl and season, add 3 tbs olive oil, and toss.

Peel and finely chop the garlic, and seed and finely chop the chilli.

Heat 1 tbs of olive oil in a thick-bottomed pan, add the garlic and when coloured, add the prawns, chilli, and season. Cook to heat through.

To make the bags, cut foil into 4 x 50cm lengths. Drizzle with olive oil. Divide the spaghetti into four, and place in the centre of each piece of foil. Spoon over 1 tbs of hot Tomato sauce, a quarter of the prawns and a few basil leaves. Bring the edges of the foil together and fold to seal, leaving the top open. Pour 2 tbs of wine into each then seal the top.

Place the bags on a tray in the oven and bake for 6-8 minutes until they inflate. Serve in the bags with lemon.

1

Penne
arrabbiata

2

Penne, mussels,
zucchini

3

Penne, sausage,
ricotta

4

Penne, zucchini,
butter

5

Rigatoni,
cabbage, fontina

6

Orecchiette,
broccoli

7

Spirale, clams,
prawns

8

Fusilli
carbonara

Short pasta

1

Penne arrabbiata

Penne	320g
Garlic cloves	2
Plum tomatoes	500g
Ex.v.olive oil	2 tbs
Dried chillies	4
Basil leaves	3 tbs

Peel the garlic and cut in half. Skin the tomatoes (see page 260) and roughly chop.

Heat the olive oil in a thick-bottomed pan and add the garlic and whole chillies. When the garlic is brown, remove with the chillies and save. Put the basil in the hot oil for a few moments to flavour it, then remove. Add the tomatoes to the olive oil and season. Cook gently for 10 minutes.

Cook the penne in boiling salted water until al dente. Drain.

Add the garlic, chilli and basil to the pasta. Stir in the tomato sauce, mixing well.

This easy arrabbiata sauce relies on flavouring the olive oil with the whole garlic pieces, whole chilli and the basil leaves before adding the tomatoes.

2

Penne, mussels, zucchini

Penne	320g
Mussels	1kg
Zucchini	500g
Garlic cloves	2
Dried chillies	2
Basil leaves	3 tbs
Parmesan	50g
Ex.v.olive oil	

Scrub the mussels. Discard any that do not close when tapped on the side of the sink.

Cut the zucchini at an angle into 5mm discs. Cut each disc into three sticks. Scatter with salt and leave to drain for 10 minutes. Pat dry. Peel and chop the garlic and crumble the chillies. Grate the Parmesan.

Heat 3 tbs of the olive oil in a thick-bottomed pan, add the zucchini and fry until brown. Add the garlic, mussels, chilli, and season. Stir and cover. Cook for 4 minutes, shaking the pan, until the mussels have opened. Add the basil. Remove half the mussels from the shells, discarding any shells that have not opened.

Cook the penne in boiling salted water until al dente, drain and add to the sauce. Stir and serve with Parmesan.

It is unusual to put Parmesan on a seafood pasta, but this Neapolitan recipe is an exception.

3

Penne, sausage, ricotta

Penne	320g
Italian sausages	4
Ricotta	100g
Tomato sauce	6 tbs
Garlic cloves	2
Onion	1
Basil leaves	3 tbs
Fennel bulb	1
Parmesan	50g
Ex.v.olive oil	1 tbs
Red wine	150ml

Make the Tomato sauce (see page 259). Peel and finely chop the garlic and onion, chop the fennel, and grate the Parmesan.

Put the sausages in a frying pan and cover with water. Bring to the boil, then simmer until the water evaporates. Cool, remove the meat from the casings and crumble with your fingers.

Fry the onion and fennel in the olive oil until soft. Add the meat, wine and the Tomato sauce, and cook for 10 minutes. Add the basil, and season.

Cook the penne in boiling salted water until al dente, then drain. Stir in the sauce.

Place a tbs of ricotta on each plate. Spoon the pasta over the ricotta, but do not combine. Serve with Parmesan.

As you eat this spicy pasta, the hidden ricotta cheese comes as a delicious soft surprise.

4

Penne, zucchini, butter

Penne	320g
Zucchini	150g
Unsalted butter	150g
Garlic cloves	2
Mint leaves	4 tbs
Parmesan	50g

Trim the ends of the zucchini, cut in half lengthways and then into approximately 1cm pieces. Peel and finely chop the garlic and chop the mint. Grate the Parmesan.

Melt half the butter in a thick-bottomed pan, add the zucchini and fry until soft. Add the garlic and season, and continue to cook, stirring, to break up the zucchini. Add the remaining butter and the mint. Smash a third of the zucchini with a fork.

Cook the penne in boiling salted water until al dente. Drain, reserving a little of the cooking water. Add it to the sauce to loosen.

Stir in the penne and serve with Parmesan.

This rich zucchini and butter sauce is a regional dish cooked in homes and trattorias from Naples to the Amalfi coast.

5

Rigatoni, cabbage, fontina

Rigatoni	320g
Savoy cabbage	1/2
Fontina	150g
Potatoes	200g
Garlic cloves	2
Anchovy fillets	6
Dried chillies	2
Nutmeg	1/2
Unsalted butter	120g
Parmesan	50g

Peel and slice the potatoes into 5mm thick discs. Peel and slice the garlic. Rinse the anchovies, crumble the chilli, and grate the cheeses and nutmeg.

Remove and discard the tough outer leaves of the cabbage. Cut into eighths and cook in boiling salted water until tender. Drain, then chop.

Melt half the butter in a thick-bottomed pan, add the garlic and fry until soft. Add the anchovies and stir to melt. Add the chilli, grated nutmeg and the cabbage.

Cook the rigatoni in boiling salted water until al dente, adding the potatoes after 6 minutes. Drain, reserving 3 tbs of the water. Add the pasta and potatoes to the cabbage and stir in the remaining butter. Add the cheese and a little of the pasta water. Cover for 1 minute to allow the cheese to melt into the sauce. Serve with Parmesan.

Fontina cheese melts easily and has a rich buttery taste. Use Gruyère as an alternative.

6

Orecchiette, broccoli

Orecchiette	320g
Broccoli	400g
Garlic clove	1
Dried chillies	3
Parmesan	50g
Ex.v.olive oil	2 tbs
Pancetta	100g

Cut the broccoli into small florets and the pancetta into matchsticks. Peel and finely slice the garlic and crumble the chilli. Grate the Parmesan.

Cook the broccoli in boiling salted water until soft.

In a thick-bottomed pan, heat the olive oil, add the pancetta and garlic, and cook until soft but not crisp. Add the broccoli and chilli, and season. Stir over a gentle heat for a few minutes.

Cook the orecchiette in boiling salted water until al dente. Drain, and add to the broccoli. Mix well, and serve with Parmesan.

It is important to cut the broccoli florets into pieces small enough to fit into the hollow of the orechiette.

7

Spirale, clams and prawns

Spirale	320g
Clams	1kg
Peeled prawns	250g
Garlic cloves	3
Fresh red chilli	1
Rocket leaves	100g
Ex.v.olive oil	
White wine	150ml

Peel and finely chop the garlic, seed and chop the chilli, and roughly chop the rocket. Wash the clams.

In a large thick-bottomed pan with a lid, heat 3 tbs olive oil and add the garlic, cook until soft, then add the clams and wine. Cover and cook until the clams have opened, about 2 minutes. Discard any that remain closed. Add the prawns, rocket and chilli and cover again to wilt the rocket. Keep warm.

Cook the pasta in boiling salted water until al dente. Drain, and add to the clams. Heat together for a minute, season and drizzle with olive oil.

Fusilli can be used as an alternative to spirale. Peeled prawns preserved in brine, or frozen, are equally good for this recipe.

8

Fusilli carbonara

Fusilli	320g
Prosciutto	300g
Parmesan	50g
Pecorino	50g
Ex.v.olive oil	1 tbs
White wine	150ml
Egg yolks, organic	5

Cut the prosciutto into 1cm strips. Finely grate the cheeses.

Heat the olive oil in a thick-bottomed pan and fry the prosciutto until soft but not crisp. Add the wine, scraping up the bits.

In a bowl combine the egg yolks and cheeses, and season.

Cook the fusilli in boiling salted water until al dente. Drain, reserving a few tablespoons of the cooking water. Add to the prosciutto, then stir in the egg mixture, letting the heat of the pasta 'cook' it. Serve with extra Parmesan.

1 Fig and chilli

2 Borlotti bean

3 Crème fraîche and rocket

4 Green bean and tomato

5 Prosciutto and radicchio

6 Dried porcini and sage

Tagliatelle

1

Fig and chilli

Egg tagliatelle	320g
Black figs	8
Dried chillies	2
Lemons	2
Parmesan	50g
Ex.v.olive oil	2 tbs
Double cream	100ml

Cut each fig into 8 pieces. Crumble the chilli. Grate the lemon peel of both lemons and squeeze the juice of one. Grate the Parmesan.

Bring a large pan of salted water to the boil and cook the tagliatelle until al dente.

While the tagliatelle is cooking, heat a frying pan large enough for the figs in one layer. Add the olive oil and when smoking, carefully place the figs in the pan, turning them immediately to caramelise. Season and add the chilli.

Drain the pasta. Stir the lemon zest and juice into the cream and mix into the tagliatelle. Add the figs and serve with the Parmesan.

Sweet ripe figs seasoned with chilli give this lemony pasta an unusual spiciness.

2

Borlotti bean

Egg tagliatelle	320g
Red onion	1
Garlic cloves	2
Pancetta	100g
Cooked borlotti	500g
Ex.v.olive oil	
Tin tomatoes	200g
Double cream	3 tbs
Basil leaves	3 tbs
Parmesan	50g

Peel and chop the onion. Peel and chop the garlic. Cut the pancetta into 1cm pieces. Rinse the beans if tinned.

Heat 2 tbs of the olive oil in a thick-bottomed pan and fry the garlic and onion until soft. Add the pancetta and cook until translucent. Add the tomatoes and cook for 5 minutes then stir in the beans and the double cream. Cook for a further 5 minutes. Add the basil and 2 tbs of olive oil. Season.

Cook the tagliatelle in plenty of boiling salted water until al dente, then drain well, retaining a little of the cooking water. Add to the sauce to loosen.

Toss the tagliatelle with the beans. Drizzle with olive oil and serve with Parmesan.

3

Crème fraîche and rocket

Egg tagliatelle	320g
Crème fraîche	250ml
Lemons	2
Rocket leaves	150g
Parmesan	150g

Finely grate the lemon peel and squeeze the juice. Roughly chop the rocket. Grate the Parmesan.

Put the crème fraîche in a bowl, stir in the lemon juice and zest, and season.

Cook the tagliatelle in boiling salted water until al dente, drain and return to the pan. Pour over the sauce, add the rocket and half the Parmesan. Toss to combine.

Serve with the remaining Parmesan.

4

Green bean and tomato

Egg tagliatelle	320g
Fine green beans	300g
Plum tomatoes	6
Parmesan	50g
Garlic clove	1
Double cream	150ml
Basil leaves	3 tbs

Top and tail the green beans, cook in boiling salted water until tender, then drain.

Cut the tomatoes in half, remove the juice and seeds and chop the flesh coarsely. Season. Grate the Parmesan.

Peel the garlic, add to the cream and bring to the boil. Season. Remove the garlic, and add the tomato, green beans and basil. Stir to combine.

Cook the tagliatelle in boiling salted water until al dente. Drain, and add to the tomato and beans. Serve with Parmesan.

This is a summer pasta. Always use the ripest tomatoes and the finest green beans.

5

Prosciutto and radicchio

Egg tagliatelle	320g
Prosciutto slices	6
Radicchio head	1
Garlic clove	1
Rosemary leaves	2 tbs
Parmesan	50g
Unsalted butter	110g

Cut the prosciutto and radicchio into ribbons the same width as the tagliatelle. Peel and finely chop the garlic. Chop the rosemary (see note below). Grate the Parmesan.

Melt half the butter in a thick-bottomed pan. Add the garlic and rosemary and cook for a minute. Add half the radicchio and prosciutto. Cook just to wilt. Remove from the heat.

Cook the tagliatelle in boiling salted water until al dente, then drain. Add the rest of the butter and half the Parmesan. Put into the cooked radicchio, then stir in the remaining radicchio and prosciutto. Toss thoroughly and serve with Parmesan.

The width of the tagliatelle you buy dictates the size of the ribbons of both the prosciutto and the radicchio. Don't pre-chop the rosemary, or it will turn black.

6

Dried porcini and sage

Egg tagliatelle	320g
Dried porcini	35g
Sage leaves	8
Garlic cloves	2
Dried chilli	1
Lemon	1
Parmesan	50g
Unsalted butter	100g
Double cream	4 tbs

Soak the porcini in 200ml of hot water for 20 minutes.

Peel and finely slice the garlic, chop the sage, and crumble the chilli. Finely grate the peel from $1/2$ lemon, and squeeze all the juice. Grate the Parmesan.

Drain the porcini, reserving the water. Rinse the porcini and chop. Strain the liquid through muslin.

Melt the butter in a thick-bottomed pan, and add the garlic, sage and chilli. Colour, then add the porcini. Fry until soft, then add 4 tbs of the liquid, and simmer until most of the juice has been absorbed. Add the cream, lemon zest and juice, and reduce until the sauce is creamy and thick. Season.

Cook the tagliatelle in boiling salted water until al dente, then drain. Add to the sauce, and turn over to coat each ribbon. Serve with Parmesan.

1 Gnudi bianchi

2 Gnudi spinaci

3 Sformata di ricotta

4 Stuffed zucchini flowers

Tutti ricotta

1

Gnudi bianchi

Ricotta	500g
Parmesan	100g
Nutmeg	1/2
Semolina flour	500g
Unsalted butter	100g
Sage leaves	3 tbs

Gnudi need to be made 24 hours before cooking.

Grate the Parmesan and nutmeg. Beat the ricotta with a fork, season and stir in the Parmesan and nutmeg.

Dust a flat tray generously with semolina flour. Roll the paste into short 8cm thick rolls in the semolina, then cut into 2.5cm pieces. Gently form the pieces into balls, coating well with the semolina, and place in the tray.

When all the gnudi are made, add more semolina in the tray so that the gnudi are slightly submerged. Leave for 24 hours in the fridge.

Just before serving put half the butter in a warm serving dish. Fry the sage leaves in the remaining butter.

Cook the gnudi in boiling salted water for 3 minutes or until they rise to the surface. Remove with a slotted spoon to the serving dish.

Serve with the sage and extra Parmesan.

'Gnudi' are just balls of ricotta rolled in semolina flour, which sticks to the surface to form a fine coat.

2 Gnudi spinaci

Ricotta	250g
Spinach	250g
Parmesan	100g
Nutmeg	1/2
Eggs, organic	3
Semolina flour	250g
Ex.v.olive oil	

Cook the spinach and drain, cool and finely chop. Grate the Parmesan and nutmeg. Separate 1 egg yolk and discard the white.

Beat the ricotta with a fork, and stir in the whole eggs one by one, then the yolk, followed by the spinach. Season, add the nutmeg and stir in the Parmesan.

Scatter a flat tray with semolina flour, and roll and shape the gnudi as in the previous recipe. You can cook them right away.

Cook the gnudi in boiling salted water for 3 minutes until they rise to the surface. Remove with a slotted spoon to a warm serving dish. Serve with extra Parmesan and a drizzle of olive oil.

Olive oil tastes the most peppery in the first three months after it has been pressed. Italian estate oils are pressed from the end of October through November, and have the production year on the label. Serve gnudi with spicy oil to contrast the sweet ricotta flavour.

3

Sformata di ricotta

Ricotta	500g
Unsalted butter	100g
Parmesan	50g
Garlic clove	1
Cherry tomatoes	300g
Ex.v.olive oil	
Eggs, organic	6
Crème fraîche	200ml
Thyme leaves	2 tbs

Preheat the oven to 200°C/Gas 6. Butter an oval ovenproof baking dish of 36 x 24cm, and grate the Parmesan. Dust the dish with Parmesan.

Peel the garlic and cut in half. Toss the tomatoes with the garlic, 1 tbs olive oil, and season. Bake for 15 minutes.

Mix the eggs and ricotta in a food processor until light. Put in a bowl and stir in the crème fraîche and half the thyme. Season.

Spoon the ricotta mixture into the baking dish, and scatter over the tomatoes and remaining thyme. Drizzle with olive oil and bake for 20 minutes.

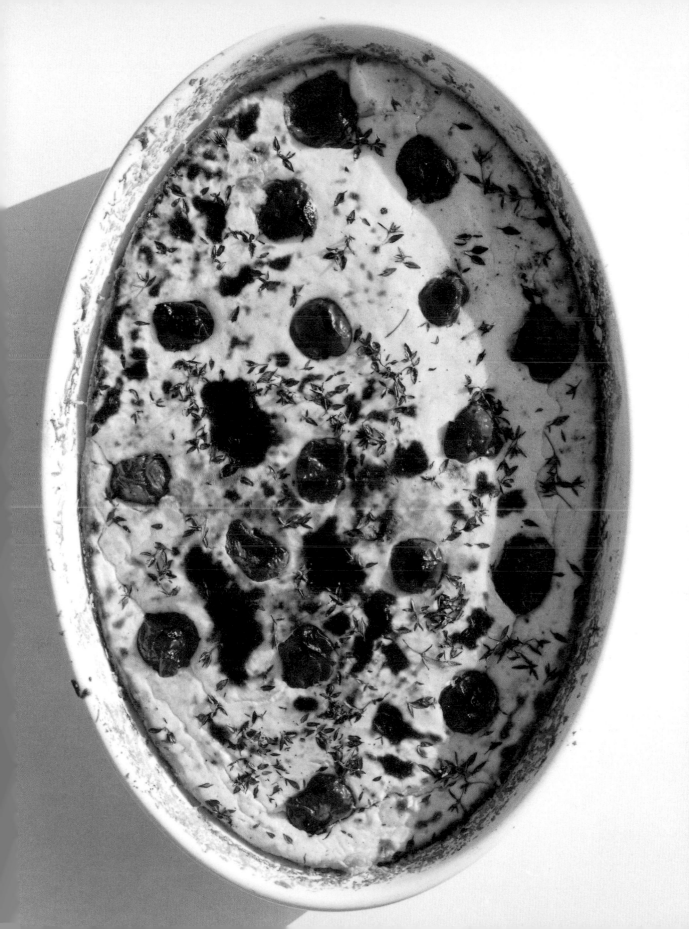

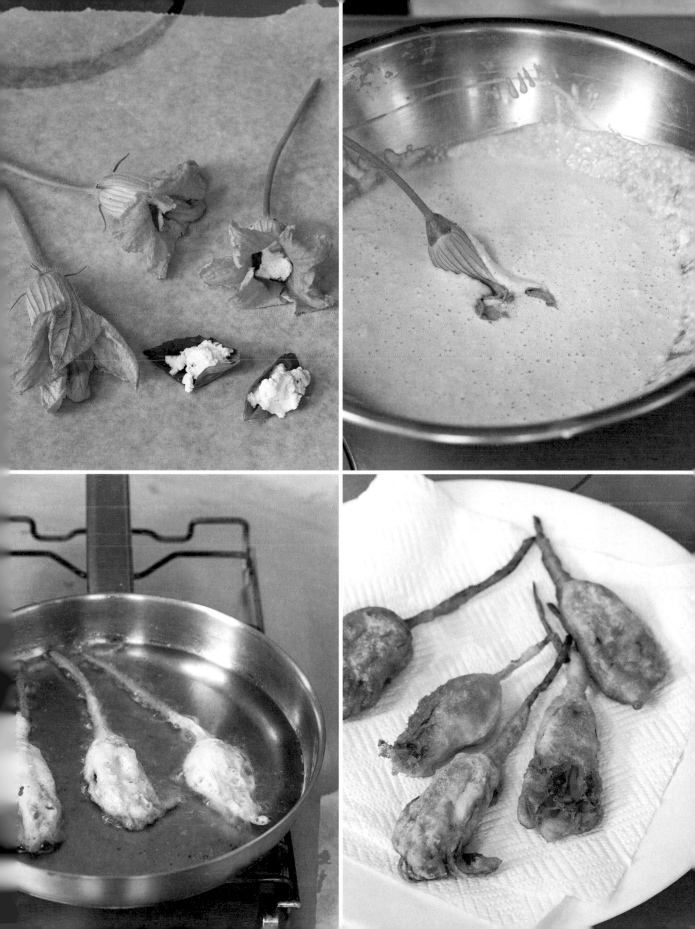

4

Stuffed zucchini flowers

Ricotta	250g
Zucchini flowers	20
Basil leaves	4 tbs
Sunflower oil	250ml
Lemons	2

Batter	
Plain flour	180g
Ex.v.olive oil	3 tbs
Egg whites, organic	3

For the first stage of the batter, sieve the flour into a bowl, make a well in the centre, pour in the olive oil and stir to combine. Loosen this paste by slowly adding enough warm water, about 200ml, to make a batter the consistency of double cream. Add 1 tsp salt, cover and leave for at least 1 hour.

To prepare the flowers, remove the stamens and the green bits at the base. Season the ricotta.

Push a tsp of ricotta and a basil leaf inside each flower. Press together.

Heat the oil to 180°C in a deep-frying pan.

Beat the egg whites until stiff, then fold into the batter.

Dip the flowers one at a time into the batter. Tap gently to knock off excess, and carefully place as many as you can without touching into the hot oil. Fry until light brown, then turn to crisp the other side.

Drain on kitchen paper. Serve with lemon.

1 Broad bean and pancetta

2 Fresh tomato

3 Asparagus and herb

4 Clam and Pinot Grigio

5 Leek and prosciutto

6 Porcini, sage and orange

7 Vin Santo with prosciutto

Risotto

1

Broad bean and pancetta

Risotto rice	250g
Broad beans	1kg
Pancetta	60g
White onion	1
Parmesan	75g
Chicken stock	1.5l
Unsalted butter	200g
Extra dry vermouth	3 tbs

Peel and finely chop the onion and cut the pancetta into matchsticks. Pod the broad beans. Grate the Parmesan.

Bring the stock to a simmer and check for seasoning.

In a thick-bottomed pan, melt half the butter, and add the onion and pancetta. Cook gently to soften, then add the rice, and stir to coat each grain with the butter. Add the vermouth, stir until it is absorbed by the rice, then add the broad beans.

Add hot stock, ladle by ladle, only adding more when the last addition has been absorbed. Stir, and continue adding the stock until the rice is cooked, about 20 minutes.

Stir in the remaining butter and Parmesan.

2

Fresh tomato

Risotto rice	250g
Tomato sauce	4 tbs
Plum tomatoes	6
Red onions	1
Garlic clove	1
Parmesan	75g
Basil leaves	5 tbs
Ex.v.olive oil	2 tbs
Chicken stock	1.5l
Unsalted butter	200g
Thyme leaves	1 tbs
Extra dry vermouth	120ml

Make the Tomato sauce (see page 259). Skin and roughly chop the tomatoes (see page 260). Peel and chop the onions and the garlic. Grate the Parmesan.

Put the tomatoes in a bowl, season, add olive oil and basil.

Bring the stock to a simmer. Check seasoning.

Melt half of the butter in a thick-bottomed pan, add the onion, cook until soft, then add the thyme and garlic. Add the rice and stir to coat each grain with the butter. Add the vermouth, stirring until it is absorbed, then add the warmed Tomato sauce. Season.

Add hot stock, ladle by ladle, only adding more when the last has been absorbed. Stir and continue adding the stock until the rice is cooked, about 20 minutes.

Remove from the heat, and stir in the marinated tomatoes, then the remaining butter and Parmesan.

3

Asparagus and herb

Risotto rice	250g
Asparagus	800g
Basil leaves	1 tbs
Parsley leaves	1 tbs
Mint leaves	1 tbs
Red onion	1
Parmesan	50g
Chicken stock	1.5l
Unsalted butter	100g
Ex.v.olive oil	3 tbs
Extra dry vermouth	75ml

Cut the tips off the asparagus, and roughly chop the stalks.

Roughly chop the parsley, mint and basil. Peel and finely chop the onion. Grate the Parmesan.

Bring the stock to a simmer. Check seasoning.

In a thick-bottomed pan melt half the butter and the olive oil. Add the onion and half the herbs and cook until soft. Add the rice, and stir to coat each grain. Add the vermouth, and stir until absorbed. Add the asparagus and stir.

Add hot stock, ladle by ladle, only adding more when the last has been absorbed. Stir and continue adding the stock until the rice is cooked, about 20 minutes.

Remove from the heat and stir in the remaining herbs, butter and Parmesan.

4

Clam and Pinot Grigio

Risotto rice	250g
Clams	1kg
Pinot Grigio	350ml
Garlic cloves	4
Dried chillies	3
Parsley leaves	3 tbs
Stock	1l
Ex.v.olive oil	3 tbs
Unsalted butter	25g
Mascarpone	150g
Lemon	1

Scrub the clams. Peel and chop the garlic, crumble the chillies and chop the parsley.

Bring the stock to a simmer. Check seasoning.

To cook the clams, heat the olive oil in a thick-bottomed pan, add half the garlic, and the chilli. Add the clams and half the wine, cover and cook to open. Discard any that do not open. Season. When cool, remove the clams from their shells, keeping them moist in their juices.

Melt the butter in a thick-bottomed pan, add the garlic and cook until lightly coloured. Add the rice and stir to coat each grain with the butter. Add the remainder of the wine, stir and reduce. Add the stock, ladle by ladle, only adding more when the last has been absorbed. Continue adding stock until the rice is cooked, about 20 minutes. In the last few minutes add the clams and their juices.

Remove from the heat and stir in the mascarpone and parsley. Serve with lemon.

Although this is a fish risotto, chicken or vegetable stock may be used.

5

Leek and prosciutto

Risotto rice	250g
Small leeks	750g
Prosciutto slices	8
Garlic cloves	2
Parmesan	50g
Basil leaves	3 tbs
Chicken stock	1.5l
Unsalted butter	225g
Pinot Nero	1 bottle

Roughly chop the leeks. Shred the prosciutto. Peel and finely chop the garlic. Grate the Parmesan.

Bring the stock to a simmer, check seasoning.

Melt half the butter in a thick-bottomed pan, add the leeks and garlic, and cook until the leeks are soft.

Add the rice and stir to combine. Add 150ml of the wine to colour and flavour the rice. Stir until reduced and then add the stock, ladle by ladle, allowing each ladle to be absorbed by the rice before adding the next, stirring all the time. After 10 minutes, add ladles of wine between ladles of stock until the rice is cooked, about 20 minutes.

Remove from the heat, and stir in the remaining butter, prosciutto, basil and Parmesan.

6

Porcini, sage and orange

Risotto rice	250g
Dried porcini	50g
Oranges	2
Sage leaves	4 tbs
Garlic cloves	2
Parmesan	60g
Unsalted butter	200g

Soak the porcini in 1 litre hot water for 1/2 hour. Remove the porcini, and keep the liquid. Rinse the porcini in a sieve under a cold tap to remove any grit. Lay on a board and roughly chop.

Grate the orange rind, squeeze the juice, and combine in a bowl. Chop the sage and add to the juice. Peel and finely chop the garlic. Grate the Parmesan.

Strain the porcini soaking liquid and heat gently. Season.

Heat half the butter in a thick-bottomed pan, add the garlic and porcini, and cook for 3 minutes to combine and soften. Add the rice and stir to coat each grain. Add a ladleful of the mushroom liquid, only adding more when the last has been absorbed. Continue adding until the rice is cooked, about 20 minutes.

Remove from the heat, stir in the orange juice and remaining butter, and half the Parmesan. Serve with the remaining Parmesan.

This is a vegetarian risotto.

7

Vin Santo with prosciutto

Risotto rice	250g
Vin Santo	350ml
Prosciutto slices	8
Red onion	1
Celery head	1
Parmesan	100g
Chicken stock	1.5l
Unsalted butter	200g

Peel and finely chop the onion, and chop the inner white heart of the celery. Grate the Parmesan.

Bring the stock to a simmer, check for seasoning.

Melt half the butter in a thick-bottomed pan. Gently fry the onion and celery until soft and beginning to colour. Add the rice and stir until each grain is coated. Add 250ml of the Vin Santo, cook and stir until it has almost been absorbed by the rice, then start to stir in the hot stock, ladleful by ladleful, only adding more stock when the last has been absorbed. Continue adding stock until the rice is cooked, about 20 minutes.

Remove from the heat and stir in the remaining Vin Santo, the butter and the Parmesan.

Serve with thin slices of prosciutto over the risotto.

1 Roasted langoustine

2 Poached langoustine

3 Mussel pangrattato

4 Crab with polenta

5 Roast whole squid

6 Monkfish spiedini

7 Grilled scallops

8 Fried scallops

9 Roast monkfish

10 Sea bass with potatoes

11 Dover sole with capers

12 Grilled tuna with fennel seeds

13 Roasted sardines

14 Red mullet with bay

15 Sicilian fish stew

Seafood

1

Roasted langoustine

Langoustines	16
Dried oregano	2 tbs
Dried chillies	3-4
Ex.v.olive oil	
Lemons	2

Preheat the oven to 220°C/Gas 7.

Cut each langoustine in half lengthways. Sprinkle the flesh side with oregano and crumbled chilli, and season. Drizzle with olive oil and squeeze over the juice of 1 lemon.

Heat a large tray and place the langoustines on it, cut side up, side by side. Roast in the preheated oven for 4-5 minutes.

Serve hot with lemon.

2 Poached langoustine

Langoustines	16
Fennel bulb	1
Celery head	1
Black peppercorns	1 tbs
Bay leaves	2
White wine	150ml
Lemons	2

Cut the fennel into quarters and the celery in half. Squeeze the lemon.

Bring a large pan of water to the boil. Add the vegetables, seasonings and wine and return to the boil. Add the langoustines, pushing them down so they are submerged. Cover and cook until the langoustines are firm, depending on the size, 3-5 minutes. Drain. Serve with Aïoli (see page 259) and lemon.

Aïoli is a perfect sauce for langoustine. Fresh red chilli sauce is also delicious and is very easy to make (see page 258).

3

Mussel pangrattato

Mussels	2kg
Garlic cloves	2
Lemons	3
Dried chilli	1
Ciabatta loaf	1/2
Oregano leaves	2 tbs
Ex.v.olive oil	4 tbs
Tin tomatoes	400g
White wine	150ml

Scrub the mussels and discard any that do not close when tapped lightly.

Peel and chop the garlic, finely grate the rind of 1 lemon, and crumble the chilli.

Remove the crust from the bread and pulse-chop in a food processor to make coarse breadcrumbs. Combine the breadcrumbs, lemon rind and half the oregano. Add just enough olive oil to hold together.

Heat the remaining olive oil in a thick-bottomed pan and fry the garlic and chilli. Add the tomatoes and remaining oregano, and cook for 5 minutes, breaking the tomatoes up. Season.

Add the mussels, stir, then add the wine. Cover the pan and raise the heat. Cook, shaking the pan, until the mussels open, about 5 minutes. Discard any that remain closed.

Divide the mussels between bowls. Scatter over the breadcrumbs, add the juices, and serve with lemon.

4

Crab with polenta

Polenta	
Polenta flour	350g
Water	1.75l
Ex.v.olive oil	3 tbs
Ex.v.olive oil	1 tbs
Garlic cloves	2
Dried chilli	2
Crab meat	500g
Flat-leaf parsley	1 tbs
Lemons	3

To make the polenta, put the polenta flour in a jug, so that it can be poured in a steady stream.

Bring the water to a boil in a thick-bottomed pan and add 1 tsp salt. Lower the heat to a simmer and slowly add the polenta flour, stirring with a whisk until completely blended. It will now start to bubble volcanically. Reduce the heat to as low as possible, and cook the polenta, stirring from time to time with a wooden spoon, for about 45 minutes. Stir in 3 tbs of olive oil and season. The polenta is cooked when it falls away from the sides of the pan and has become dense and thick.

While the polenta is cooking, crush the chilli and peel and chop the garlic and chop the parsley.

Heat 1 tbs of the olive oil in a frying pan. Add the garlic and cook until soft. Stir in the chilli and crab. Cook quickly, to heat the crab through. Add the parsley. Season. Squeeze over the juice of $1/2$ lemon.

Spoon the polenta on to warm plates, and serve with the crab mixture. Drizzle over olive oil, and serve with lemon.

In Venice, fish and polenta are often served together.

5

Roast whole squid

Squid	1kg
Dried chillies	3
Ex.v.olive oil	
Dried oregano	1 tbs
Lemons	2

Preheat the oven to 220ºC/Gas 7.

To prepare the squid, hold the body in one hand and gently pull away the head and tentacles, with the soft pulp inside the sac. Cut off the tentacles and squeeze out the beak. Feel inside the body and pull out the quill. Wash the tentacles and the inside and outside of the body. Keep on the fins and skin. Pat dry.

Crumble the chilli.

Heat an oven tray and brush with olive oil. When the olive oil is very hot, put in the squid and tentacles. Scatter over the oregano and chilli, and season.

Squeeze over the juice of $1/2$ lemon, and drizzle with a little olive oil. Put in the oven and roast for 5 minutes.

Serve with lemon.

6

Monkfish spiedini

Monkfish	800g
Fennel herb	2 tbs
Ex.v.olive oil	3 tbs
Pancetta slices	12
Lemons	2

Cut the monkfish into 16 x 3cm cubes.

Chop the fennel. Put the monkfish in a bowl with the fennel, and season. Add the olive oil and stir. Marinate in the fridge for 15 minutes.

Preheat the barbecue, griddle pan or grill.

Fold the pancetta into 3, approximately the same size as the monkfish. Using wood, metal or rosemary stick skewers, thread on the monkfish, alternating with the pancetta: four pieces of fish and three of pancetta per skewer.

Grill the spiedini carefully, turning from time to time. This should take about 8 minutes.

Serve with lemon.

7

Grilled scallops

Scallops	16
Lemons	2
Ex.v.olive oil	

Preheat the grill, griddle pan or barbecue.

Season the scallops very generously on both sides with salt and pepper. Place on the grill until lightly brown and crisp, then turn over and grill on the other side. The scallops should be tender on the inside, crisp on the surface.

Serve with lemon and a drizzle of olive oil.

Anchovy and rosemary sauce (see page 258) goes well with all kinds of grilled fish.

8

Fried scallops

Shelled scallops	12
Anchovy fillets	8
Ex.v.olive oil	
Lemons	2

Season the scallops on both sides. Tear the anchovy fillets in half.

Heat a thick-bottomed frying pan large enough to hold the scallops in one layer. When very, very hot, carefully place the scallops in to sear on each side. This will take seconds.

Add 1 tbs olive oil to the pan, place the anchovies amongst the scallops, and squeeze over the juice of 1 lemon. Fry for 1 minute until the anchovies become crisp.

Serve drizzled with olive oil, with lemon.

9 Roast monkfish

Monkfish tail	2kg
Lemons	2
Ex.v.olive oil	
Rosemary sprigs	2
Anchovy fillets	8

Preheat the oven to 220°C/Gas 7.

Cut 1 of the lemons across into fine slices. Season and drizzle with oil.

Heat an ovenproof tray, and drizzle with olive oil. Place the rosemary sprigs on the tray, and the fish on top. Cover with lemon slices and the anchovies. Season.

Roast in the oven until cooked. To test, pierce with a pointed knife; the juices should be opaque. Large monkfish will take 20-30 minutes.

Serve with lemon.

For this recipe, buy whole monkfish tail on the bone. Ask the fishmonger to remove the tough outer skin. A tail weighing 500g is ideal for one person, and it will cook in less time.

10

Sea bass with potatoes

Sea bass	2kg
Waxy potatoes	800g
Black olives	80g
Ex.v.olive oil	
Capers	60g
Thyme leaves	3 tbs
Dry white wine	150ml

Preheat the oven to 200°C/Gas 6.

Peel the potatoes and boil until just cooked in salted water. Cut them lengthways into 5cm slices. Stone the olives. Rinse the capers.

Line a baking tray with baking parchment, drizzle with olive oil, and cover with the potatoes. Place the fish on top, and scatter over olives, capers and thyme. Push some inside the fish, and season.

Put in the oven, and after 5 minutes pour over the wine and a little more oil. Bake until the fish is cooked, about 20 minutes.

Fillet the bass and divide into 4. Serve the fish portion with potatoes, olives, capers and the fish juices poured over.

11

Dover sole with capers

Dover sole	4
Capers	2 tbs
Ex.v.olive oil	
Marjoram leaves	2 tbs
Lemons	2

Preheat the oven to 220°C/Gas 7.

Wash the salt from the capers.

Heat 2 flat oven trays, scatter them with salt and pepper, and drizzle with olive oil. Place the fish on the trays, skin-side down.

Scatter over the capers and marjoram, season and drizzle with olive oil.

Put the trays into the oven and roast the fish for 10-15 minutes or until the flesh comes easily away from the bone when tested with a knife.

Serve with lemon.

12

Grilled tuna with fennel seeds

Tuna loin	800g
Fennel seeds	2 tbs
Dried chillies	2
Lemon	1
Ex.v.olive oil	

Preheat the barbecue, grill or griddle pan.

Cut the tuna into 4 equal steaks. Crush the seeds and crumble the chilli.

Season each steak with the fennel, chilli, salt and pepper. Place on or under the grill. Cook for a minute or so, then turn over and grill the other side. Squeeze the juice of the lemon over the fish and drizzle with oil.

Tuna steak is best eaten rare in the centre, crisp on the outside. If you are cooking on a charcoal barbecue, grill close to the coals a minute on each side. If using a griddle pan, make sure it's very, very hot, and turn the steak clockwise two or three times to make criss-cross sear marks before turning over to grill the other side.

13

Roasted sardines

Sardines	24
Cherry tomatoes	500g
Ex.v.olive oil	
Black olives	50g
Lemons	4

Preheat the oven to 200°C/Gas 6.

Pierce the tomatoes with a fork. Toss with olive oil, season and bake for 15 minutes.

Stone the olives and grate the peel of 2 lemons.

Use an ovenproof dish large enough to hold the sardines in one layer, and drizzle with olive oil. Place the sardines in, side by side, and season. Sprinkle over the lemon zest, olives and tomatoes, and drizzle with olive oil. Bake for 10 minutes. Serve with lemon.

14

Red mullet with bay

Red mullet	4
Fresh bay leaves	40
Garlic cloves	4
Ex.v.olive oil	lots
Lemons	2

Ask the fishmonger to leave the livers in when cleaning the fish, as they add delicious flavour.

Wash the bay. Peel and slice the garlic into slivers.

Make 3 cuts into one side of each fish, and push in a bay leaf and a piece of garlic. Do the same on the other side. Place a few bay leaves inside each fish and season. Put in a dish and pour over a generous amount of olive oil. Cover and marinate for $^1/2$ hour or longer.

Preheat the oven to 220°C/Gas 7.

Put the mullet in an ovenproof tray. Cover with the remaining bay. Place foil over loosely and bake for 20 minutes, removing the foil during the last few minutes. Serve with lemon.

420-450g is the ideal weight of fish per person.

15

Sicilian fish stew

Mussels	500g
Red mullet fillets	500g
John Dory fillets	300g
Garlic cloves	3
Coriander seeds	1 tbs
Fennel seeds	1 tbs
Tin chopped tomatoes	400g
Ex.v.olive oil	
Dry white wine	250ml
Mint leaves	2 tbs
Ciabatta loaf	1
Lemons	2

Fish stock	
Fish bones	250g
Bay leaves	2
Garlic cloves	2
Fresh red chillies	2
Dry white wine	150ml

For the stock, put the fish bones in a thick-bottomed pan with the bay leaves, peeled garlic, chillies, wine and 400ml water, and season. Bring to the boil and skim. Simmer for 10 minutes, then strain and put aside.

For the stew, scrub the mussels. Peel and chop 2 garlic cloves, and grind the coriander and fennel seeds.

In a thick-bottomed pan, heat 2 tbs olive oil, add the garlic and colour. Add the seeds and tomatoes, and season. Cook, breaking up the tomatoes, for 10 minutes. Remove from the heat and purée.

Return to the pan and bring to the boil. Add the stock. Add the mussels, mullet and Dory. Pour in the wine and season. Cover and cook until the mussels open and the fish is cooked, about 5 minutes. Discard any mussels still closed.

Chop the mint. Cut the ciabatta into slices. Toast on both sides, rub with the remaining garlic, place in soup bowls and pour over the fish and the broth. Add the mint and a drizzle of olive oil, and serve with lemon.

1
Chicken with nutmeg

2
Chicken in milk

3
Chicken with lemon

4
Flattened chicken

5
Boiled chicken

6
Guinea fowl with fennel

7
Grouse with bruschetta

8
Spiced pigeon

9
Pheasant with potatoes

10
Roast quail with sage

11
Grilled partridge

12
Duck with tomatoes

Birds

1

Chicken with nutmeg

Organic chicken	1.5kg
Lemon	1
Nutmeg	1/2
Prosciutto slices	4
Ex.v.olive oil	
White wine	125ml

Preheat the oven to 190°C/Gas 5.

Wipe the chicken clean and trim off all excess fat. Cut the lemon in half. Grate the nutmeg.

Rub the chicken all over with the lemon, squeezing the juice into the skin. Season the skin and inside the cavity with salt, pepper and nutmeg. Tuck the prosciutto slices into the cavity.

Put the chicken on an oven tray, breast-side down, drizzle with olive oil and roast for 1^1/2 hours, basting from time to time. Add the wine after ^{1}/2 hour. Turn the bird breast-side up for the last 20 minutes.

Serve with the juices from the pan.

This is a simple roast chicken recipe. The unusual combination of spicy nutmeg with the prosciutto stuffing gives it a festive quality.

2

Chicken in milk

Organic chicken	1.5kg
Garlic cloves	6
Lemon	1
Milk	500ml
Unsalted butter	80g
Sage leaves	8-10

Wipe the chicken clean and trim off all the excess fat. Peel the garlic.

Cut the lemon in half. Rub the chicken all over with lemon, squeezing the juice into the skin and cavity. Season inside and out.

Heat the milk to boiling point.

Melt the butter in a thick-bottomed pan large enough to hold the chicken, and brown the chicken on all sides. Add the garlic and sage, and fry for a minute. Put the chicken on its side, and add the milk to come halfway up the chicken. Simmer with the lid at half tilt, for 1 hour. Baste the uncovered side from time to time. Turn the chicken on to its other side after $1/2$ hour.

The milk will reduce to make a thick, curdled sauce.

This chicken is also delicious cold.

3

Chicken with lemon

Organic chicken	1.5kg
Lemon	1
Thyme leaves	4 tbs

Preheat the oven to 200°C/Gas 6.

Wipe the chicken clean and trim off all excess fat. Wash the lemon and thyme.

Squash the lemon, then pierce all over with a cooking fork until soft.

Season the chicken skin and the cavity. Put the lemon and the thyme inside, and close using wooden toothpicks.

Roast the chicken on an oven tray, breast-side down, for 1^1/$_2$ hours. Do not use any oil or butter, the chicken will self-baste. Turn the bird breast-side up after the first hour.

Serve with the juices.

4

Flattened chicken

Organic chicken	1.5kg
Garlic cloves	4
Thyme leaves	3 tbs
Ex.v.olive oil	
Lemons	1¹/2

Preheat the oven to 200°C/Gas 6.

Wipe the inside of your flattened chicken and trim off any fat. Lay the chicken out, skin-side down, on a board. Using your finger, gently prise the skin away from the meat, creating pockets.

Peel the garlic and finely chop with the thyme, adding 1 tbs salt. Push this mixture into the pockets and scatter the remainder over the surface. Turn the chicken over and use the seasoning that has fallen off to rub into the skin side.

Drizzle an oven tray with olive oil. Lay the chicken skin-side up. Squeeze over the juice of ¹/2 lemon, and drizzle with olive oil. Roast for 30-40 minutes, basting occasionally with the juices from the pan and the remaining lemon juice.

Carve by cutting across the chicken in thick slices.

This recipe is only easy if you can get your butcher to bone the chicken for you. Ask to have it boned out through the back bone, keeping the breast in one piece, removing the carcass and the leg bones.

5

Boiled chicken

Organic chicken	2kg
Celery heads	2
Young carrots	12
Potatoes	500g
Thyme sprigs	2
Bay leaves	3-4
Black peppercorns	2 tbs

Gremolata	
Garlic cloves	2
Parsley leaves	3 tbs
Lemon	1

Wipe the chicken clean and trim off all excess fat. Cut the hearts of the celery into quarters. Wash and scrub the carrots. Peel and halve the potatoes.

Bring a large thick-bottomed pan of water to the boil. Add the thyme, bay, peppercorns, 2 potatoes, and salt.

When the water returns to the boil, add the chicken. Lower the heat and simmer very gently for 25 minutes. Add the remaining potatoes, the celery hearts and carrots, and continue to simmer until the vegetables are tender and the chicken is cooked, about 30-40 minutes

For the gremolata, peel and chop the garlic, chop the parsley, grate the lemon peel, and combine.

Check the seasoning of the chicken stock and add the lemon juice. Smash some of the potatoes into the stock. Carve the chicken into 8 pieces and put into large soup bowls, with the vegetables and plenty of stock. Stir in the gremolata.

6

Guinea fowl with fennel

Guinea fowl	2
Garlic cloves	4
Rosemary leaves	2 tbs
Red onion	1
Fennel bulbs	3
Ex.v.olive oil	
Pancetta slices	10
White wine	250ml

Ask the butcher to cut up each guinea fowl into 8 pieces. Wipe the pieces clean and trim off any fat.

Peel and finely chop the garlic and chop the rosemary. Peel the onion, and cut the onion and fennel into eighths. Cut the pancetta into 1cm pieces.

Preheat the oven to 200°C/Gas 6.

Mix the garlic and rosemary with salt and pepper. Put the guinea fowl into a bowl, drizzle with olive oil and add the garlic mixture. Turn each piece over to thoroughly coat.

Put the guinea fowl in one layer in a roasting tin and scatter the fennel, red onion and pancetta over. Drizzle with olive oil and roast for 1/2 hour.

Add the wine and roast for a further 20 minutes. Raise the heat to 225°C/Gas 9 for the last few minutes to brown.

7

Grouse with bruschetta

Grouse	4
Thyme sprigs	16
Unsalted butter	200g
Ex.v.olive oil	1 tbs
Red wine	350ml
Sourdough loaf	1/4
Garlic clove	1

Preheat the oven to 220°C/Gas 7.

Stuff each grouse with 4 sprigs of thyme and a knob of butter. Season the outside of the grouse and inside of each cavity.

Put the birds breast-side down in an oven tray. Drizzle over the olive oil.

Pour over a glass of the red wine. Roast for 10 minutes. Turn the birds breast-side up, pour over a second glass of wine and cook for a further 10 minutes, basting with the wine juices. Finally add the remaining wine and butter and roast for 5 minutes. Remove from the oven.

Cut the bread into 4 thick slices. Grill on both sides and rub lightly with the peeled garlic.

Press the garlic side of each piece into the juices in the pan, and turn them over on to hot plates. Place the grouse on top and pour over the remaining juices.

There is nothing more delicious than this wine/grouse-flavoured bruschetta, especially when served with a bitter leaf salad such as watercress, chicory or dandelion. Grouse cooked for 25 minutes will be medium, not rare.

8

Spiced pigeon

French pigeons	4
Garlic cloves	4
Dried chillies	2
Coriander seeds	1 tbs
Tin chopped tomatoes	400g
Ex.v.olive oil	2 tbs
Cinnamon stick	1
Red wine	350ml
Nutmeg	½

Preheat the oven to 180°C/Gas 4.

Peel and halve the garlic cloves, crumble the chilli, and grind the coriander seeds.

Season the pigeon insides with salt, pepper, coriander and chilli.

Heat a thick-bottomed casserole large enough to hold all 4 pigeons, add the olive oil, and when hot, brown on each side. Add the garlic, cinnamon, tomatoes and wine, then grate in the nutmeg. Season.

Bring to the boil, then put into the oven and roast uncovered until the legs pull away easily, about 45 minutes.

Roasted squash (see page 212) goes very well with pigeon cooked in this way.

9

Pheasant with potatoes

Hen pheasants	2
Potatoes	500g
Pancetta slices	12
Garlic cloves	4
Unsalted butter	100g
Sage leaves	2 tbs
Chianti Classico	350ml

Preheat the oven to 180°C/Gas 4.

Wipe the pheasants clean and trim off the fat. Peel the potatoes, and cut into 4 lengthways. Cut the pancetta into 1cm pieces, keep back 4 slices. Peel and cut the garlic in half lengthways. Tie 2 pancetta slices over each bird with string to secure. Season the cavity.

Heat half the butter in a thick-bottomed casserole large enough to hold the pheasants. Brown the birds on each side. Remove from the pan, pour out the butter and wipe the pan with kitchen paper.

Melt the remaining butter in the pan, and add the garlic, sage and pancetta. Cook to soften. Add the potatoes and stir to combine. Add the pheasants, pour over the wine and bring to the boil. Cover and cook in the oven for 35 minutes.

10

Roast quail with sage

Organic quail	12
Sage leaves	5 tbs
Sea salt	5 tbs
Ex.v.olive oil	
Lemons	2

Preheat the oven to 200°C/Gas 6.

Wipe the quail dry. Roughly chop the sage with the salt. Completely smother the quail inside and out with this mixture.

Heat a roasting tray on top of the stove, brush with olive oil, and brown the birds on all sides. Put in the oven and roast until the legs come easily away from the breast and the skin is crisp. The quails should be almost overcooked. This will take at least 1/2 hour.

Serve with lemon.

Organic quail are usually larger than farmed, and taste 100% better. Allow 3 per person. Quail cooked in this way are good for a party – you can eat them with your fingers.

11

Grilled partridge

Grey-legged partridge	4
Ciabatta loaf	$^1/_2$
Dried chillies	2
Lemons	2
Ex.v.olive oil	3 tbs

Remove the crusts from the bread. Pulse the bread to fine breadcrumbs in a food processor. Crumble the chillies. Halve 1 of the lemons.

With scissors, cut away the backbone of each partridge to open the bird out flat. The easy way is to cut either side of the backbone where the thin ribs join. Push the bird flat with the ball of your hand.

Season the partridges with salt, pepper and chilli. Drizzle over olive oil, and turn the birds. Add the breadcrumbs, turning the birds so that they are fully coated in the breadcrumbs. Leave for $^1/_2$ hour.

Preheat the barbecue, griddle pan or grill.

Grill the partridge, turning frequently, and squeeze the lemon halves over from time to time.

Partridge take up to 25 minutes to cook to slightly pink.

Serve with lemon.

12

Duck with tomatoes

Duck	1
Cherry tomatoes	350g
Black olives	100g
Red wine	300ml

Preheat the oven to 220°C/Gas 7.

Wipe the duck dry, pull out excess fat, and prick the thick fatty bits of the skin using a skewer, particularly the area between legs and breast. Rub the skin with salt and pepper, and season the insides. Stone the olives.

Put the duck on a rack in a roasting tray, breast-side up, and roast on the lowest shelf of the oven for 20 minutes. Turn the duck over and roast for a further 1/2 hour.

Lower the heat to 200°C/Gas 6 and pour out the fat, and roast for a further 15 minutes, breast-side up. Pour out any remaining fat, add the tomatoes, olives and wine, and roast for a further 15 minutes.

Let the duck rest for about 10 minutes before carving. Spoon the tomatoes and olives over each serving.

The tomatoes and wine make a thick tangy sauce which goes well with this crisp roast duck.

1 Beef steak
Fiorentina

2 Arista di
maiale

3 Leg of lamb
with garlic

4 Veal
chops

5 Pork chops
with lemon

6 Grilled fillet
of beef

7 Cotechino
lentils

8 Sausage
and wine

9 Lamb chops
scottadito

Veal, lamb, pork, beef

1

Beef steak Fiorentina

T-bone steak	2.5kg	Preheat a barbecue, chargrill or large griddle pan.

Season the steak generously. Place on the grill and seal on all sides. As the steak is so thick, you must turn it frequently to prevent it from burning. It will be rare in some parts and better done in others. This will take about 15 minutes.

Carve the meat, giving each person slices of both fillet and sirloin.

T-bone steak is a cut of beef on the bone which combines the fillet and the sirloin. One thick steak around 6cm thick, weighing approximately 2.5kg, is perfect for 4 people.

2

Arista di maiale

Pork loin, boned	1.5kg
Dried chillies	2
Garlic cloves	4
Sea salt	1 tbs
Fennel seeds	2 tbs
Ex.v.olive oil	1 tbs
White wine	250ml

Ask the butcher to bone out the ribs and backbone, keeping the fillet intact and leaving a little of the belly flap. Remove the skin and some of the fat from the back. The loin will look flat, but don't have it tied up.

Preheat the oven to 200°C/Gas 6.

Crumble the chilli. Pound the peeled garlic with salt and fennel seeds to a soft paste. Rub this into all parts of the meat. Season with black pepper and chilli. Roll the meat up, wrapping the belly flap up round the fillet. Tie to secure with butcher's string every 2-3cm.

Heat the olive oil in a roasting tray and brown the loin on all sides. Put in the oven and roast for 20 minutes. Add the wine, baste, and continue to roast for a further $1/2$ hour, or until the meat feels firm when pressed. Remove from the oven and allow to rest for 5 minutes. Skim off any fat, turn the pork over and baste whilst resting.

Remove the string and serve cut in thick slices with the juices.

In Italy the butchers often leave the rib bones in the roll, sticking up like a rake.

3

Leg of lamb with garlic

Leg of lamb	3kg
Garlic cloves	8
Ex.v.olive oil	
Milk	200ml

Preheat the oven to 210°C/Gas 6^1/$_2$.

Peel and cut the garlic cloves into slivers. With the sharp point of a knife, make slits in the fat of the lamb and insert the garlic. Rub the lamb with olive oil, salt and pepper, and put in a roasting tray. Put into the oven and roast for 15 minutes. Lower the heat to 150°C/Gas 2, and cook for a further 3 hours until the meat is tender and can be cut with a fork.

Remove the lamb from the tin and put on a warm plate. Skim the fat off the juices, and put the pan over a medium heat. When very hot, add the milk, stirring and scraping up all the bits stuck to the pan. Lower the heat and cook until the sauce is a nutty brown colour. Serve the sauce with the lamb.

4

Veal chops

Veal loin chops	4
Garlic cloves	4
Sage leaves	4 tbs
Lemon	1
Ex.v.olive oil	2 tbs

Peel the garlic and chop finely. Chop the sage, and grate the lemon peel. Mix together with salt and pepper.

Put the chops in a bowl, add the olive oil and squeeze in the juice of 1/2 lemon. Add the garlic mixture, turn the chops over and marinate for 1 hour.

Preheat a barbecue, chargrill or large griddle pan.

Brush most of the garlic and herbs off the chops and pat dry with kitchen towel before grilling.

Put the chops on the grill and allow to brown lightly. Turn them over to brown on the other side. Squeeze a little lemon juice over whilst they cook. Turn the chops frequently so that they cook evenly. Chops 3cm thick will take between 10 and 15 minutes.

Chops cooked this way need to be really thick. Each should weigh about 500-600g.

5

Pork chops with lemon

Pork loin chops	4
Lemon	1

Preheat an ovenproof griddle pan. Pre-heat the oven to 200°C/Gas 6.

Season each chop, put on the griddle pan, and seal on each side.

Cut the lemon in half. Heat an oven tray. Put in the chops, squeeze over the lemon juice, and place the squeezed lemon halves in the tray. Roast in the oven for 10 minutes. Press the lemon halves on to the chops and baste with the juice. Roast for another 10 minutes or until firm to the touch.

Grilling the pork chops first gives them an interesting, charred flavour. Roasting the lemon with the chops and squeezing the cooked juices over the meat will result in a delicious lemony sauce to pour over at the end. Pork chops should be cut 3cm thick. Serve with Salsa rossa piccante (see page 259) or Salsa verde (see page 258).

6

Grilled fillet of beef

Fillet of beef	1.5kg
Red wine	350ml
Lemon	1

Trim and season the fillet and put into a bowl. Pour over the wine, cover and leave to marinate for an hour. Turn over from time to time.

Preheat a griddle pan to very hot.

Cut the fillet across into 1cm slices. Stretch the pieces of meat out to expand, and season. Place the slices on the griddle pan to brown on each side. This will take only 2-3 minutes.

Serve 3-4 slices per person with a rocket salad and lemon.

Buy the fillet in one whole piece and use a very sharp knife when slicing. Once marinated, the beef will keep up to 24 hours in the fridge. Beef cooked this way is delicious with fresh Horseradish sauce (see page 258) and the Fresh borlotti bean salad (see page 38).

7

Cotechino lentils

Cotechino sausages	2
Lentils	250g
Garlic clove	1
Ex.v.olive oil	
Lemon	1
French mustard	2 tbs
Mustard fruits	

Cook the cotechino in the foil packages as directed on the box. Cotechino will take approximately $1/2$ hour to cook. Slice into 1cm thick slices.

For the lentils, put in a thick-bottomed pan with the peeled garlic, cover with water, and cook for 20 minutes. Drain and return to the pan. Stir in 3 tbs of olive oil, the juice of $1/2$ lemon, the mustard, salt and pepper.

Divide the lentils between 4 warm plates, and put the cotechino slices on top.

Serve with Mustard fruits (see page 230) and Salsa verde (see page 258).

Mustard fruits are a northern Italian preserve of candied fruits in a strong mustard-flavoured syrup, traditionally served with Bollito misto (see suppliers' list, page 263).

8

Sausage and wine

Italian sausages	6
Red wine	350ml
Onion	1
Celery	1
Carrots	2
Parsley leaves	2 tbs
Sage leaves	2 tbs
Garlic cloves	2
Cloves	3
Dried chillies	2
Ex.v.olive oil	
Tin tomatoes	400g

Cut the sausages into 2cm slices. Peel the onion. Chop the onion, celery heart and carrot into small pieces. Chop the parsley and sage, peel and finely chop the garlic, grind the cloves and crumble the chillies.

Heat a thick-bottomed frying pan, brush with oil, add the sausage and fry gently to release the fat and brown on each side. Remove from the pan, and pour away the fat. Add 1 tbs of olive oil to the pan, then the chopped vegetables, and fry until lightly coloured.

Add the garlic, sage, cloves and chilli. Stir to combine. Add the drained tomatoes and the wine, and cook for 20 minutes over a medium heat until thick. Return the sausages to the pan and simmer gently for a further 10 minutes. Season.

Serve with polenta (see page 126) or Mashed potatoes with Parmesan (see page 192).

Quick-cook polenta is more convenient but has less flavour than traditional polenta, which is easy to make, but takes 50 minutes (see page 126).

9

Lamb chops scottadito

Neck end lamb chops 16
Pork lard 150g
Ex.v.olive oil 3 tbs
Lemons 2

Trim all the fat from the chops, and place the chops on a board. Using a flat-bladed knife, press to flatten out the meat as thin as you can, enlarging it to twice its size.

Melt the lard in the olive oil over a gentle heat. Dip in each chop to coat. Place on kitchen paper to cool, which will solidify the lard.

Heat a large flat frying pan until very hot. Lay in the chops side by side; you will have to do this in batches. Season, and brown. Turn over. This will only take 2 minutes on each side.

Serve the chops in a pile with lemon halves. Eat with your fingers while still hot.

1 Roast potatoes in a pan

2 Potato and fennel

3 Potatoes and mustard

4 Stuffed pumpkin

5 Potatoes with lemon

6 Potato gnocchi

7 Gnocchi with prosciutto

8 Gnocchi with tomato sauce

9 Mashed potatoes

Potatoes

1

Roast potatoes in a pan

Waxy potatoes	600g
Rosemary leaves	2 tbs
Garlic cloves	3
Ex.v.olive oil	

Peel and cut the potatoes into 2cm cubes. Chop the rosemary. Peel and cut the garlic cloves in half.

Heat a thick-bottomed pan with a lid. Add sufficient olive oil to cover the bottom. When very hot, add the potatoes, rosemary and garlic, season generously and cover.

Cook over a medium high heat, shaking the pan to prevent them from sticking. Make sure the potatoes are turned over so they become crisp and brown on all sides. This will take 15 minutes.

This recipe is for roast potato lovers who do not have an oven in their kitchen. It is a very traditional Italian recipe and is often on the menu in Tuscan trattorias.

2

Potato and fennel

Waxy potatoes	600g
Fennel bulbs	600g
Parmesan	100g
Garlic cloves	6
Ciabatta loaf	1/2
Lemon	1
Double cream	250ml
Unsalted butter	100g

Preheat the oven to 200°C/Gas 6.

Remove the outer part of the fennel and chop the leafy tops. Slice the bulbs in half lengthways and each half into four. Peel the potatoes and slice lengthways into similar-sized pieces. Grate the Parmesan. Peel the garlic.

Make breadcrumbs with the ciabatta (see page 260), and combine with 1 tbs of Parmesan and the fennel tops.

Cook the fennel and potatoes in boiling salted water with the peeled garlic and lemon juice for 8 minutes. Remove the fennel and potatoes, leave the garlic.

Discard all but 6 tbs of the cooking water. Add the cream and boil until the liquid thickens. Mash in the garlic and add the remaining Parmesan.

Mix the potatoes and fennel together, and season. Pour in the sauce, mix well, and put into a buttered baking dish. Dot butter on top, and bake in the oven for 1/2 hour. Sprinkle the breadcrumbs over, dot with more butter and bake until brown.

3

Potatoes and mustard

New potatoes	1kg
Parsley leaves	4 tbs
Capers	2 tbs
French mustard	2 tbs
Ex.v.olive oil	6 tbs
Red wine vinegar	1 tbs

Scrub the potatoes and cook in salted water until tender. Drain.

Chop the parsley finely, and rinse and chop the capers.

Put the potatoes in a salad bowl and mix in half the parsley and capers.

In a small bowl combine the mustard and vinegar, then slowly add the olive oil drop by drop, whisking to a thick consistency, like mayonnaise. Season and gently stir into the potatoes. Scatter over the remaining parsley. Serve warm.

Stuffed pumpkin

Potatoes	500g
Small pumpkins	2
Dried chillies	2
Pancetta	150g
Garlic cloves	3
Ex.v.olive oil	
Thyme leaves	2 tbs

Preheat the oven to 220°C/Gas 7.

Peel the potatoes and cut into 2cm cubes. Crumble the chilli, and cut the pancetta into matchsticks. Peel and finely chop the garlic.

Cut off and discard the top 1/4 of each pumpkin, and scoop out the seeds. Season the insides with salt, pepper and chilli, and put on an oven tray lined with foil. Drizzle generously over and inside the pumpkins with olive oil and bake for about 15 minutes.

Boil the potatoes for 8 minutes. Drain, place in a bowl, and add the pancetta, thyme and garlic. Season, stir and drizzle with a little olive oil.

Spoon into the part-baked pumpkins, and return to the oven for a further 30-40 minutes. Test by sticking a fork into the side of each pumpkin. The flesh should be soft and almost falling apart.

The best small pumpkin for this recipe is the common Onion squash, ideally 10cm in diameter.

5

Potatoes with lemon

Waxy potatoes	500g
Garlic cloves	2
Lemons	2
Marjoram leaves	4 tbs
Ex.v.olive oil	

Preheat the oven to 220°C/Gas 7.

Scrub and cut the potatoes in half lengthways, and each half again lengthways. Peel and chop the garlic.

Cut the lemons in half lengthways, and each half into three and each third in half. Put in a bowl with the potatoes, squeezing the juice out of the lemon pieces with your hands as you mix.

Add the garlic, marjoram, salt and pepper, and enough olive oil to moisten well. Tip into an ovenproof dish.

Roast for $1/2$ hour, until they are cooked and brown. Halfway through, turn the pieces over.

This is a good summer recipe. Its unusual lemony flavour makes it delicious hot or cold.

6

Potato gnocchi

White floury potatoes   1kg
Plain flour   250g
Unsalted butter   100g

Wash the potatoes and keep them whole. Cook with their skins on, in boiling salted water until soft, about 20 minutes, depending on size. Peel and whilst hot, immediately put through a mouli or potato ricer on to a clean surface.

Sift over the flour, season and combine rapidly, to form a smooth, soft and elastic dough.

Roll into sausage-like rolls of about 1.5cm in diameter, and cut into pieces about 2-3cm long. Press each piece against the prongs of a fork to form little ridges – these will help hold the sauce.

Cook the gnocchi in boiling salted water for 3 minutes or until they rise to the surface. Remove with a slotted spoon to a warmed dish.

Melt the butter until just soft, and combine with the gnocchi. Season and serve with Parmesan.

7 Gnocchi with prosciutto

Basic gnocchi recipe	1
Swiss chard leaves	300g
Garlic cloves	2
Ex.v.olive oil	3 tbs
Prosciutto slices	3

Blanch the chard in boiling salted water. Drain, cool, then chop roughly. Peel and chop the garlic.

Heat 2 tbs of olive oil in a thick-bottomed pan and fry the garlic until soft. Add the chard, and season.

Cook the gnocchi as before, but omit the butter. Mix the chard with the gnocchi. Tear over small pieces of the prosciutto and drizzle over olive oil and sprinkle with Parmesan.

8 Gnocchi with tomato sauce

Basic gnocchi recipe	1
Red onions	3
Garlic cloves	2
Basil leaves	3 tbs
Ex.v.olive oil	2 tbs
Tin tomatoes	2 x 400g

Peel and slice the onions as thinly as possible into rounds. Peel and finely slice the garlic.

Heat the olive oil in a wide thick-bottomed pan, then add the onion and garlic. Cook over a low heat until very soft, but not brown. Add the tomatoes, and stir to break them up, then season. Cook slowly over a low to moderate heat, stirring occasionally, for at least an hour. Remove from the heat and stir in the basil.

Cook the gnocchi as before, but omit the butter. Serve with the tomato sauce, sprinkled with Parmesan

9

Mashed potatoes

Potatoes	600g
Parmesan	40g
Nutmeg	1/2 tsp
Unsalted butter	45g
Milk	6 tbs

Peel the potatoes and cut in half. Grate the Parmesan and nutmeg. Soften the butter.

Cook the potatoes in boiling salted water until soft. Heat the milk to boiling point.

Drain and mash the potatoes. Beat in the butter, milk and nutmeg, then fold in the Parmesan and season.

The best potatoes to use for this recipe are a floury variety such as King Edward or Maris Piper.

1 Zucchini fritti

2 Whole zucchini

3 Swiss chard

4 Peas and prosciutto

5 Spinach and balsamic

6 Green beans and tomatoes

7 Broad beans and peas

8 Cauliflower, fennel seeds

9 Slow-cooked fennel

10 Grilled tomatoes

11 Dried plum tomatoes

12 Slow-roast tomatoes

13 Grated zucchini

14 Grilled radicchio

15 Roasted squash

Verdura

1

Zucchini fritti

Zucchini	500g
Sunflower oil	1l
Batter	
Plain flour	150g
Ex.v.olive oil	3 tbs
Warm water	3 tbs
Egg whites, organic	3

Cut the zucchini into 5mm thick ovals, then cut them into thick matchsticks. Place in a colander, sprinkle with salt, and leave for $1/2$ hour.

For the batter, sieve the flour into a bowl, make a well in the centre, pour in the olive oil and stir to combine. Loosen this paste by slowly adding enough warm water to make a batter the consistency of double cream. Leave for $1/2$ hour. Season.

Heat the oil in a high-sided pan to 190ºC.

Beat the egg whites until stiff and fold into the batter.

Pat the zucchini dry, dip them in the batter, then fry in batches in the hot oil until golden and crisp. Serve immediately

This is a recipe where you can make good use of large zucchini.

2

Whole zucchini

Zucchini	500g
Garlic cloves	2
Lemon	1
Basil leaves	3 tbs
Ex.v.olive oil	3 tbs

Boil the whole zucchini in salted water until tender. Drain. Trim the ends and cut lengthways in half. Put in a colander and leave for $1/2$ hour, pressing gently to remove excess water. Place in a salad bowl.

Peel and chop the garlic finely and squeeze the lemon. Tear the basil.

In a bowl combine the garlic, lemon juice and olive oil. Season, then mix into the zucchini. Scatter over the basil.

3

Swiss chard

Swiss chard	1.5kg
Lemons	2
Ex.v.olive oil	6 tbs

Wash the chard, cut the stalks from the chard and chop into 2cm pieces. Wash the leaves and stalks, keeping them separate.

Boil the chard stalks until tender in salted water. Remove with a slotted spoon and drain well.

Return the water to the boil and cook the chard leaves for 5 minutes. Drain.

Squeeze the lemons, add the olive oil, and season. Dress the stalks and the leaves separately.

4

Peas and prosciutto

Fresh peas	2kg
Spring onions	4
Garlic cloves	2
Unsalted butter	100g
Prosciutto slices	150g

Pod the peas, and roughly chop the white part of the spring onions. Peel and chop the garlic.

Melt half of the butter in a frying pan, add the onions and garlic, and cook slowly to soften. Do not let them brown.

Add the peas, stir to combine, then add the remaining butter and season. When the peas are tender, after about 10 minutes, add the prosciutto, turn off the heat, cover and leave for 5 minutes. Serve warm.

5

Spinach and balsamic

Spinach	1.5kg
Ex.v.olive oil	4 tbs
Balsamic vinegar	2 tbs

Remove any tough stems from the spinach. Wash well.

Boil the spinach in salted water for 3 minutes, then drain. Press gently to remove excess moisture.

Whilst warm, season, then add the olive oil and balsamic vinegar.

6

Green beans and tomatoes

Ripe tomatoes	300g
Fine green beans	500g
Garlic cloves	2
Basil leaves	2 tbs
Ex.v.olive oil	

Skin the tomatoes (see page 260) then halve, squeezing out juice and seeds. Cut the stalk end from the green beans. Peel and finely slice the garlic. Tear the basil.

Heat 2 tbs of the olive oil in a thick-bottomed pan, and brown the garlic. Add the tomatoes, season, cover and cook for 15 minutes on a medium heat.

Boil the beans in salted water until soft, about 10 minutes. Drain, then stir into the tomato sauce. Season and drizzle with olive oil. Add the basil.

7

Broad beans and peas

Broad beans	1kg
Peas	1kg
Spring onions	150g
Spinach	500g
Ex.v.olive oil	5 tbs

Pod the broad beans and peas, and roughly chop the white part of the onions. Remove the tough stems from the spinach, and wash.

Heat 3 tbs olive oil in a thick-bottomed pan, add the onion and soften. Add the peas and broad beans and enough water to just cover. Season and cook slowly until the peas and broad beans are soft, and the liquid has been absorbed.

Boil the spinach in salted water. Drain and roughly chop.

Add the spinach to the peas and beans and cook for 5 more minutes to combine the flavours. Season, and drizzle with olive oil.

8

Cauliflower, fennel seeds

Cauliflower	1 large
Cherry tomatoes	300g
Dried chillies	2
Garlic cloves	2
Fennel seeds	2 tsp
Basil leaves	3 tbs
Ex.v.olive oil	3 tbs

Cut the white centre stem from the cauliflower and discard. Break the head into florets. Slice each floret in half lengthways. Cut the tomatoes in half and squeeze out the seeds. Crumble the chilli, and peel and finely slice the garlic.

Heat a thick-bottomed pan with a lid, add the olive oil, garlic, chilli and fennel seeds. Cook until the garlic has slightly coloured, then add the cauliflower. Stir to combine the flavours and lightly brown.

Add the tomatoes, season, cover and cook gently for 10-15 minutes. Stir in the basil.

You could add extra spice with fresh ginger and a few crushed coriander seeds.

9   Slow-cooked fennel

Fennel bulbs	8
Garlic cloves	4
Dried chillies	2
Fennel seeds	1 tsp
Ex.v.olive oil	

Cut the outer leaves and stalks from the fennel, then cut each in half and each half into four. Keep the leafy tops. Peel and cut the garlic cloves in half. Crumble the chillies. Grind the fennel seeds.

Heat a thick-bottomed pan with a lid, add the olive oil, the fennel, fennel seeds, chilli and season. Stir over a high heat until the fennel begins to colour, then add the garlic. Lower the heat. Cover and cook quickly for 10-15 minutes until the fennel is soft.

Check for seasoning, then stir in the leafy fennel tops and drizzle with olive oil.

In Italy, extra virgin olive oil is often added to cooked vegetables just before serving, as a seasoning.

10

Grilled tomatoes

Plum tomatoes	500g
Ex.v.olive oil	
Balsamic vinegar	

Preheat the barbecue or a griddle pan to very hot.

Cut the tomatoes in half lengthways. Generously scatter a plate with salt and pepper and press the cut side of each tomato into the mixture.

Put the tomato halves, seasoned side down, on the grill for 2-3 minutes until charred. Carefully turn over – they will be quite soft – and grill briefly on the skin side. Place on a serving dish, charred side up, and drizzle with olive oil and a few drops of balsamic vinegar.

This way of cooking tomatoes is only suitable for fleshy varieties such as beef steak or plum that have less juice and seeds.

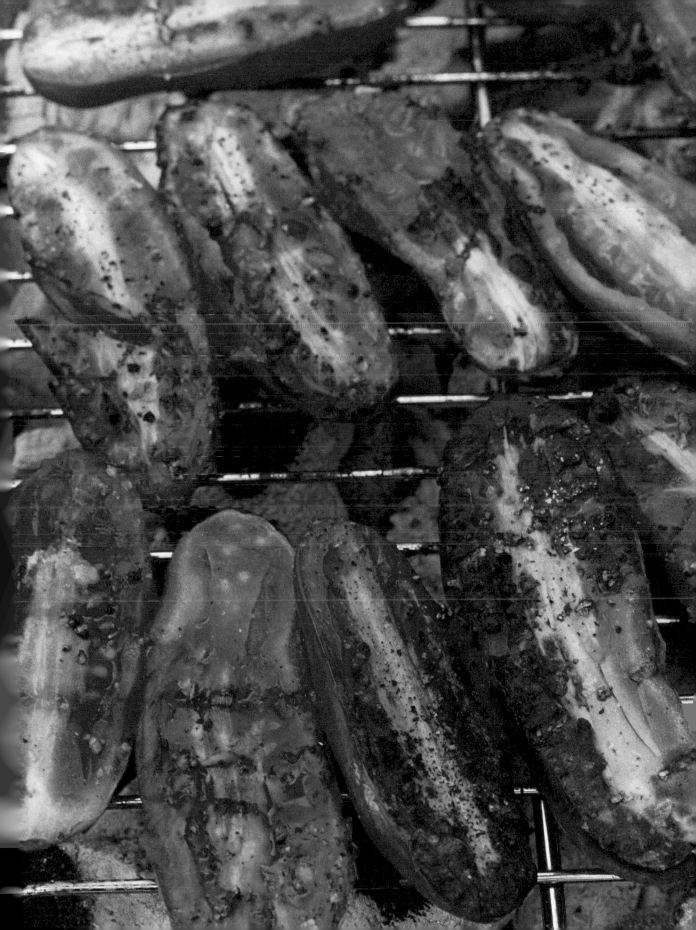

11

Dried plum tomatoes

Plum tomatoes	12
Ex.v.olive oil	
Marjoram leaves	3 tbs

Skin the tomatoes (see page 260), keeping them whole. Preheat the oven to the lowest heat.

Lightly oil a baking tray. Put the tomatoes side by side, season and drizzle with olive oil. Bake in the low oven for 2-2$^1/_2$ hours, gently pressing every $^1/_2$ hour to release the juices so that the tomatoes dry up and become concentrated in flavour.

Serve at room temperature drizzled with olive oil and scattered with marjoram.

Only make this recipe with ripe, plum tomatoes when they are at their best in mid-summer. Other varieties will have too much juice and won't achieve the intense flavour.

12

Slow-roast tomatoes

Cherry tomatoes	600g
Garlic cloves	4
Dried oregano	2 tbs
Ex.v.olive oil	3 tbs

Preheat the oven to 160-170°C/Gas 3. Prick the tomatoes with a fork. Peel and halve the garlic. Put the tomatoes, oregano, garlic and olive oil in an ovenproof tray and season. Roast for 40 minutes. Serve at room temperature.

13

Grated zucchini

Zucchini	1kg
Nutmeg	1/2
Parsley leaves	2 tbs
Garlic clove	1
Ex.v.olive oil	

Wash the zucchini, dry, then grate them on the large holes of a cheese grater. Place in a colander, spread out and sprinkle with salt. Leave for 1/2 hour to release water. Wrap in a clean towel and wring out the water.

Grate the nutmeg. Finely chop the parsley. Peel and finely chop the garlic.

Heat 2 tbs of the olive oil in a thick-bottomed pan, add the zucchini, nutmeg, garlic, and season. Cover and cook on a medium heat for 3 minutes. Add the parsley, and stir to combine. Drizzle with olive oil.

14

Grilled radicchio

Radicchio heads	3
Lemons	2
Ex.v.olive oil	
Balsamic vinegar	

Preheat a grill or griddle pan.

Cut the radicchio into halves through the stalk, then cut each half into eight segments through the stalk to keep the leaves attached.

Put the radicchio on the grill briefly, just to wilt. Remove and place in a serving dish.

Season generously and drizzle with lemon juice, olive oil and balsamic vinegar.

Try serving Grilled radicchio with Grilled scallops (see page 130) – the bitter flavour contrasts with the sweetness of the scallops.

15

Roasted squash

Squash	1kg
Garlic cloves	2
Dried chilli	¼ tsp
Fennel seeds	1 tsp
Dried oregano	1 tbs
Thyme leaves	1 tsp
Ex.v.olive oil	

Preheat the oven to 200ºC/Gas 6.

Peel the squash. For Butternut, cut in half lengthways, remove the seeds, then cut each half into quarters. For Delicate, cut in half lengthways, remove the seeds and cut each half in half. For Onion, cut in half lengthways then cut into eighths.

Peel and chop the garlic, crumble the chilli, and crush the fennel seeds.

Put the squash in a bowl with the garlic, chilli, fennel, oregano, thyme, and season. Add olive oil to coat each piece.

Put the squash on an oven tray. Bake for 20 minutes. Turn over and bake for a further 10 minutes or until the pieces of squash are cooked and lightly brown.

The skin of squash varies: at the beginning of the season, October, it is still soft, so keep it on when roasting. In December and January the skin should be removed, as it becomes hard. Onion squash are the small, round, bright orange squash with quite dry deep orange flesh. Delicate squash are oblong, striped and taste like potatoes. Butternut squash are flesh coloured and have a soft, juicy texture when cooked.

1
Wild
strawberries

2
Peaches in
Pinot Nero

3
Raspberries
with ricotta

4
Orange
ice cream

5
Fig
sorbet

6
Lemon
ice cream

7
Fig
ice cream

8
Tartufo
gelato

9
Peach and
lemon sorbet

10
Blackberry
sorbet

11
Strawberry
granita

12
Mascarpone
sorbet

13
Marsala
ice cream

14
Roasted almond
ice cream

15
Crème
anglaise

16
Pears in
mustard syrup

Fruit & ice cream

1

Wild strawberries

Wild strawberries
Lemons
Caster sugar

Squeeze lemon juice and stir with the sugar until dissolved. Pour over the wild strawberries, and marinate for $1/2$ hour, gently turning the fruits over in the juice.

Serve with caster sugar sprinkled over the top.

We have not given amounts of lemon and sugar, as it depends on how many wild strawberries you have. We usually allow a punnet per person, and $1/2$ lemon and a tablespoon of sugar per punnet.

2

Peaches in Pinot Nero

White peaches	6
Pinot Nero	1 bottle
Lemons	2
Caster sugar	6 tbs

Halve the peaches and remove the stones. Cut the lemon peel in pieces, making sure you remove any bitter white pith.

Cut the peaches into slices 3mm thick. Put in a deep bowl, sprinkle with sugar, cover with the wine, and add the lemon peel. Cover with clingfilm and leave to marinate for an hour in a cool place.

Serve in wine glasses.

This is an unusual recipe for marinating peaches, as they are not peeled and are marinated in red wine rather than white. Find a young Pinot Noir (Pinot Nero in Italian) and choose ripe, firm peaches.

3

Raspberries with ricotta

Raspberries punnets	4
Ricotta	250g
Lemon	1
Caster sugar	4 tbs

Finely grate the lemon peel and mix with the sugar. Leave for a while to allow the flavours to combine and the sugar to be absorbed.

Scatter the raspberries on a large plate. Turn the ricotta very carefully out of the tub, and then slice it as finely as possible. Place these ricotta slices carefully over the raspberries. Sprinkle with the lemon sugar.

Supermarkets sell pasteurised cows' milk ricotta in 250ml tubs. Specialist cheese shops may have fresh sheep's or goats' milk ricotta; it is usually made in 1kg baskets and sold by the slice, and should be eaten within a few days of being made.

4

Orange ice cream

Oranges	8
Lemon	1
Caster sugar	200g
Double cream	500ml
Grand Marnier	4 tbs

Finely grate the rind of the oranges and the lemon, and put in a bowl. Add the juice of 2 oranges and leave to steep.

Squeeze the juice of the remaining oranges, combine with the sugar and cook to reduce to a thick syrup. Cool.

Whip the cream to soft peaks. Stir in the reserved juice and rind to the syrup. Add the juice of the lemon, and stir into the cream. It will immediately thicken. Add the Grand Marnier.

Freeze in a shallow container, stirring every 1/2 hour or so, or churn in an ice cream machine.

5

Fig sorbet

Black figs	12 very ripe
Lemon	1
Caster sugar	200g
Double cream	150ml

Squeeze the lemon. Peel the figs, leaving some skin. Put them with the lemon juice in a food processor and chop coarsely. Put in a bowl and stir in the sugar and cream.

Freeze in a shallow container, stirring every 1/2 hour or so, or churn in an ice cream machine.

6 Lemon ice cream

Lemons	3
Caster sugar	200g
Double cream	450ml
Salt	1/2 tsp

Finely grate the peel of 1 of the lemons. Squeeze the juice of all 3 and combine with the sugar. Slowly add the cream and salt, mixing carefully. It will immediately thicken.

Pour into a shallow container and freeze until solid around the outside and mushy in the middle. Stir with a fork and freeze until firm, or churn in an ice cream machine.

7 Fig ice cream

Black figs	8
Dark brown sugar	3 tbs
Lemon	1/2
Crème anglaise	300ml

Put the figs into a bowl and pour over boiling water just to colour the skin. Remove from the water and dry. Cut off the stalks and chop roughly. Add the sugar and lemon juice. Stir to mix.

Stir into the Crème anglaise (see page 227). Freeze in a shallow container, stirring every 1/2 hour or so, or churn in an ice cream machine.

Ready-made crème anglaise is fine to use for this ice cream.

8

Tartufo gelato

Chocolate 100%	220g
Chocolate 70%	220g
Milk	600ml
Egg yolks, organic	4
Caster sugar	100g
Double cream	5 tbs

Break the chocolate up into small pieces. Keep separate. Heat the milk.

In a bowl, whisk the egg yolks with the sugar until thick, then add the hot milk, whisking all the time. Put in a thick-bottomed pan and cook over a low heat, stirring until the mixture thickens and coats the back of a spoon. Remove from the heat.

Melt the 100% chocolate with half the 70% chocolate in a bowl over simmering water. Remove from the heat, and slowly add the hot custard, whisking all the time. Cool.

Stir in the cream. Churn in an ice cream machine or freeze in a shallow container. About 5 minutes before it is frozen, mix in the remaining pieces of 70% chocolate, and continue churning or freezing until set.

The 100 per cent cocoa solids chocolate is so bitter it is inedible on its own, but is essential to this recipe. In Rome you will find this ice cream in the 'Tre Scalini' gelateria in the Piazza Navona.

9

Peach and lemon sorbet

Yellow peaches	6
Lemon	1
Caster sugar	200g

Peel, stone and chop the peaches. Finely grate the peel and squeeze the lemon. Combine with the sugar and leave for $1/2$ hour. Freeze in a shallow container, stirring every $1/2$ hour or so, or churn in an ice cream machine.

10

Blackberry sorbet

Blackberries	500g
Caster sugar	350g
Water	150ml
Lemon	$1/2$

Combine the sugar and water and cook to reduce to a thick syrup. Squeeze the lemon. Pulse the blackberries in a food processor. Add the syrup and lemon juice. Freeze in a shallow container, stirring every $1/2$ hour or so, or churn in an ice cream machine.

11

Strawberry granita

Strawberries	500g
Caster sugar	200g
Balsamic vinegar	1 tbs
Lemon	$1/2$
Water	50ml

Make a sugar syrup with the water and 150g sugar. Cool and add the vinegar.

Squeeze the lemon. With a fork, smash the strawberries with the remaining sugar. Add the lemon juice, and mix with the syrup. Freeze in a shallow container, stirring every $1/2$ hour or so, or churn in an ice cream machine.

It is only worth making this granita if you have a sweet and thick, aged balsamic vinegar.

12

Mascarpone sorbet

Mascarpone	250g
Lemon	1
Caster sugar	200g
Water	350ml

Squeeze the lemon. Make a thick sugar syrup with the sugar and water. Add the lemon juice. Put the mascarpone into a bowl and stir with a whisk to lighten. Stir in the syrup. Freeze in a shallow container, stirring every $1/2$ hour or so, or churn in an ice cream machine.

13

Marsala ice cream

Egg yolks, organic	10
Caster sugar	200g
Dry Marsala	350ml
Double cream	450ml

Beat the yolks with the sugar until light and fluffy. Add 100ml of the Marsala and transfer to a bowl that will fit over a thick-bottomed pan of simmering water. The water should not touch the bowl. Stir until the mixture comes up to the boil. This will take $1/2$ hour. Stir in the remaining Marsala. Cool.

If using an ice cream machine, just add the cream and churn. If not, beat the cream before folding into the mixture, then freeze in a shallow container, stirring every $1/2$ hour or so.

Extra dry sherry is a good alternative to Marsala.

14

Roasted almond ice cream

Blanched almonds	250g
Crème anglaise	500ml
Unsalted butter	15g
Caster sugar	2 tbs

Preheat the oven to 180°C/Gas 4.

Make the Crème anglaise (see below). Place the almonds on a flat oven tray and bake until lightly brown. Add the butter and sugar, mix and bake for a further 10 minutes. Cool.

Put the almonds on half a kitchen cloth, fold the other half over, and bash into bits with a rolling pin. Stir the almonds into the Crème anglaise. Freeze in a shallow container, stirring every 1/2 hour or so, or churn in an ice cream machine.

15

Crème anglaise

Double cream	400ml
Milk	125ml
Vanilla pods	1
Eggs organic	4
Caster sugar	90g

Separate the eggs. Scrape the vanilla. In a thick-bottomed pan combine the milk, the vanilla seeds and the cream. Cook until just boiling.

Beat the egg yolks and sugar until pale and thick.

Pour the warm cream/milk slowly into the egg yolks and stir. Return to the saucepan and cook over low heat stirring constantly. When it is at almost boiling point remove from heat. If it boils, the sauce will curdle. Let cool.

16

Pears in mustard syrup

William pears	2kg
Dry white wine	1 bottle
Caster sugar	400g
Mustard essence	1 tsp

Peel the pears. Cut each pear in half lengthways, remove the core and cut each half into six.

Put the pears with the wine and sugar in a bowl, pressing them down into the marinade. Cover with clingfilm touching the surface of the wine, and leave for 10 hours in the fridge.

Remove the pears from the marinade. Put the marinade into a thick-bottomed pan, bring to the boil, and reduce by half to a thick syrup. Add the mustard essence and stir.

Add the pears to the hot syrup. Heat your jam jars and fill with the pears. Cover and seal. Once opened keep in a fridge and eat within two weeks.

We ate mustard fruit at a wedding in Parma and were given the recipe for pears. This recipe is also suitable for apples and quinces, just follow the same procedure. The challenge is to find the mustard essence (see suppliers' list, page 263).

1 Ricciarelli 2 Ciambelline 3 Amaretti

Italian biscuits

1

Ricciarelli

Blanched almonds	250g
Candied orange peel	30g
Plain flour	25g
Caster sugar	120g
Water	40ml
Egg whites, organic	2
Icing sugar	2 tsp
Baking powder	1½ tsp

Rolling out
Cornflour	100g
Icing sugar	200g
Rice paper sheets	2

Put almonds, peel and flour in a processor and mix to a sticky paste.

Combine the caster sugar and water, and cook, reducing to a thick syrup. Cool.

Mix the paste with the syrup and leave covered in the fridge for 2 hours.

Preheat the oven to 110°C/Gas ¼.

Beat the egg whites with the icing sugar until stiff. Mix with the paste to loosen, then add the baking powder.

Scatter a surface very generously with a mixture of icing sugar and cornflour. Roll the paste, incorporating some of the mixture, into a soft flat roll 6cm thick. Cut into slices 1cm thick.

Put the slices on baking trays lined with rice paper. Scatter over icing sugar. Bake in the oven for ½ hour. The biscuits will rise and have a cracked surface and a chewy centre. Sprinkle with icing sugar before serving.

The rice paper will stick firmly to the bottom of the biscuits, just tear off the paper from around them.

2

Ciambelline

Red wine	225ml
Ex.v.olive oil	225ml
Caster sugar	200g
Plain flour	
Aniseed	2 tsp

Put the wine, olive oil and sugar into a bowl. Sieve in as much flour as you need to make a stiff dough.

Pound the seeds and add half to the dough. Mix to distribute them evenly and wrap the dough in clingfilm. Rest for $1/2$ hour.

Preheat the oven to 160°C/Gas 3.

Divide the dough into small pieces of golf-ball size, and roll out into little finger-thick rolls. Cut into 6cm lengths. Make each length into a loop, pinching the ends together. Scatter over the remaining seeds.

Line a tray with parchment paper and brush with olive oil. Put on the biscuits and bake for 40 minutes, or until crisp. Remove and cool on a rack.

This recipe comes from the Capezzana estate outside Florence. Fennel seeds may be used instead of the aniseed. The biscuits are traditionally served with a glass of Vin Santo.

3

Amaretti

Blanched almonds	300g
Caster sugar	300g
Egg whites, organic	5

Preheat the oven to 180°C/Gas 4.

Put the almonds in a mortar and add 100g of the sugar little by little, pounding constantly. This step is important, in order to extract the oil from the almonds.

Beat the egg whites until stiff. Fold in the remaining sugar and add the almonds.

Cut ribbons of greaseproof paper 5cm wide, and put on a baking tray. Put teaspoonfuls of the mixture on, about 2cm apart.

Sprinkle with sugar and bake for 20 minutes.

1 Plum and orange

2 Pistachio

3 Pine nut

4 Polenta crumble

Almond cakes

1

Plum and orange

Plums

Ripe plums	500g
Orange	1
Caster sugar	50g
Vanilla pod	1

Cake

Unsalted butter	150g
Caster sugar	150g
Eggs, organic	2
Self-raising flour	85g
Baking powder	1/2 tsp
Blanched almonds	100g

Topping

Orange	1
Unsalted butter	30g
Muscovado sugar	25g
Flaked almonds	50g

Finely grate the rind and squeeze the juice of the orange. Grind the almonds in a food processor.

Preheat the oven to 180°C/Gas 4.

Halve and stone the plums and put in an ovenproof dish with the sugar, the orange juice and rind. Add the split vanilla pod and bake for 20 minutes. Cool. Scrape in the vanilla seeds.

Grease a 25cm round spring-form tin, lined with parchment paper, with extra butter.

Soften the butter and beat with the sugar until light and fluffy. Beat in the eggs one by one. Fold in the flour, baking powder and ground almonds.

Pour into the tin and push the plums and their juices into and over the cake. Bake in the oven for 1/2 hour.

For the topping, finely grate the orange rind. Melt the butter and stir in the sugar, zest and flaked almonds. Spread this over the half-baked cake, lower the heat to 160°C/Gas 3 and bake for a further 20 minutes. Cool the cake in the tin.

2

Pistachio

Unsalted butter	270g
Lemon	1
Vanilla pod	1
Blanched almonds	100g
Pistachios	120g
Caster sugar	250g
Eggs, organic	4
Plain flour	40g

Topping	
Lemon	1
Pistachios	60g
Caster sugar	50g

Preheat the oven to 150°C/Gas 2.

Line a loaf tin of 30 x 9cm, and 8cm deep, with parchment paper, and grease with 20g of the butter.

Soften the remaining butter. Finely grate the lemon peel. Split the vanilla pod and scrape the seeds. Finely grind the almonds and pistachios together.

Beat the butter and the sugar until light and fluffy. Beat in the eggs, one at a time. Add the zest, vanilla seeds, then fold in the nuts and sieve in the flour.

Spoon the mixture and bake for 45 minutes-1 hour. The cake is ready when a skewer comes out clean. Leave to cool in the tin, then turn out.

For the topping, grate the lemon peel and squeeze the juice. Halve the pistachios. Mix the lemon juice with the sugar, boil until thick, then add the zest. Stir in the pistachios and pour over the cake.

3

Pine nut

Unsalted butter	250g
Vanilla pod	2
Lemons	2
Pine nuts	6 tbs
Caster sugar	220g
Eggs, organic	4
Plain flour	100g
Ground almonds	120g
Salt	1/4 tsp

Preheat the oven to 150°C/Gas 2.

Line a loaf tin 22 x 12cm, and 6cm deep, with parchment paper, and grease with extra butter.

Soften the butter. Scrape the seeds out of the vanilla pods. Finely grate the lemon peel. Juice 1 of the lemons. Roughly chop half the pine nuts.

Beat the butter and sugar with the vanilla seeds until light and fluffy, then stir in the eggs one at a time. Fold in the flour, ground almonds and chopped pine nuts, and stir in the lemon peel and juice.

Mix the remaining pine nuts with the salt. Spoon the mixture into the tin, sprinkle over the salted pine nuts and bake in the oven for 1 hour. The cake is ready when a skewer comes out clean. Leave to cool in the tin.

Adding a little salt to the pine nuts for the top of the cake gives them a more interesting flavour.

4

Polenta crumble

Unsalted butter	120g
Plain flour	120g
Lemon	1
Blanched almonds	120g
Polenta	140g
Caster sugar	120g
Egg yolks, organic	2

Preheat the oven to 180°C/Gas 4. Butter and flour a 20cm round cake tin, using extra butter and flour.

Soften the butter. Finely grate the lemon peel and grind the almonds coarsely. Put the lemon peel and almonds in a bowl with the flour, polenta and sugar. With a fork, mix in the egg yolks, and then the butter. You should have a crumbly dough.

Press this dough into the prepared tin and bake for $1/2$ hour. Let it cool completely before cutting.

1 Dark truffle

2 Walnut and brandy

3 15 minute

4 Espresso and hazelnut

5 Easy small nemesis

Chocolate cakes

1

Dark truffle

Chocolate 70%	225g
Double cream	300ml
Cocoa powder	2 tbs

Break the chocolate into pieces, and melt in a bowl over simmering water.

Warm the cream, then stir into the warm chocolate. Place a 15cm cake ring on a flat plate. Pour the mixture into the ring and leave to set for 1 hour in the fridge.

To remove the ring, soak a dish cloth in very hot water and wrap it around the ring for 2 minutes to slightly melt the edges of the cake, making it easy to turn out.

Shake the cocoa powder over the top.

2

Walnut and brandy

Chocolate 70%	250g
Unsalted butter	350g
Shelled walnuts	300g
Eggs, organic	4
Caster sugar	220g
Brandy	3 tbs

Using extra butter, grease a 25cm cake tin, and line with parchment paper. Preheat the oven to 160°C/Gas 3.

Chop the walnuts in a food processor until the consistency of fine breadcrumbs. Break the chocolate into pieces and melt with the butter in a bowl over a pan of simmering water.

Separate the eggs. Beat the yolks with the sugar until pale. Slowly add the melted chocolate, then fold in the walnuts. Beat the egg whites until stiff and fold into the mixture. Pour into the tin.

Bake in the oven for 10 minutes. Reduce the heat to 150°C/Gas 2 and bake for a further 45 minutes. Cool in the tin.

When cool, turn out and pour the brandy over the cake.

3

15 minute

Chocolate 70%	450g	
Unsalted butter	215g	
Eggs, organic	6	

Preheat the oven to 220°C/Gas 7. Using extra butter, grease a 25cm spring-form cake tin, and line with parchment paper.

Break the chocolate into pieces, and melt with the butter in a bowl over simmering water.

In a separate bowl, over simmering water, beat the eggs until they start to thicken, then remove from the heat and continue beating until firm peaks form.

Fold half the eggs into the melted chocolate, then fold in the remainder. Pour the mixture into the tin and cover with buttered foil.

Place in a bain-marie of very hot water. It is essential, if the cake is to cook evenly, that the water comes halfway up the sides of the tin.

Bake for 5 minutes, remove the foil, and bake for a further 10 minutes until just set. Remove from the water and cool in the tin. Turn out when completely cool.

The butter, chocolate and eggs should all be at room temperature.

If using an electric mixer, warm the bowl and beat close to the stove,

while the chocolate is melting.

4

Espresso and hazelnut

Unsalted butter	300g
Shelled hazelnuts	480g
Instant coffee	4 tbs
Chocolate 70%	180g
Eggs, organic	6
Caster sugar	220g

Preheat the oven to 160°C/Gas 3.

Using extra butter, grease a 25cm cake tin, and line with parchment paper.

Roast the hazelnuts in the oven until brown. Let cool, rub off the skins and grind them to a fine powder.

Dissolve the instant coffee in 1 tbs of hot water.

Break the chocolate into pieces and melt with the butter and coffee in a bowl over simmering water. Cool, then fold in the hazelnuts.

Separate the eggs and beat the yolks and sugar in a mixer until pale and doubled in size. Fold in the chocolate.

Beat the egg whites until stiff, and then carefully fold into the mixture. Pour into the tin.

Bake in the oven for 40 minutes. Cool in the tin.

5

Easy small nemesis

Chocolate 70%	340g
Unsalted butter	225g
Eggs, organic	5
Caster sugar	210g

Preheat the oven to 120°C/Gas $1/2$.

Using extra butter, grease a 25cm cake tin, and line with parchment paper.

Break the chocolate into pieces and melt with the butter in a bowl over simmering water. Beat the eggs and 70g of the sugar in an electric mixer until the volume quadruples.

Heat the remaining sugar with 100ml water until dissolved into a light syrup. Pour the hot syrup into the melted chocolate and cool slightly.

Add the chocolate to the eggs, and beat slowly until the mixture is combined. Pour into the tin.

Put a folded kitchen cloth in the bottom of a baking tray. Put in the cake and add enough hot water to come three-quarters of the way up the side of the tin.

Bake in the oven for 50 minutes until set. Leave the cake to cool in the water before turning out.

Chocolate

All the best chocolate is made up of pure cocoa solids and sugar, sometimes with the addition of natural vanilla, and cocoa butter for extra smoothness; avoid chocolate with non-cocoa vegetable fats. The amount of cocoa solids is now written as a percentage on the label of most bars. When choosing chocolate for making cakes and ice creams, aim for a cocoa solids content between 55 and 75 per cent. A high percentage of cocoa solids does not, however, always guarantee high quality chocolate. Good brands to look for are Rococo, Valrhona, El Rey, Amedei, and Green and Black's Organic.

To melt chocolate, place in a bowl over a pan of simmering water; the water should not touch the bowl. Store chocolate in a cool dry place between 16-18°C – never in the fridge.

1 Fresh red chilli

2 Anchovy and rosemary

3 Horseradish

4 Salsa verde

5 Aïoli

6 Salsa rossa piccante

7 Quick tomato

8 Coarse breadcrumbs

9 Peeling tomatoes

10 Salted anchovies

11 Dried chickpeas

12 Dried borlotti and cannellini beans

Sauces & basics

1 Fresh red chilli

Fresh chillies	6
Ex.v.olive oil	5 tbs

Cut the chillies in half lengthways, scrape out the seeds and finely chop. Season generously and cover with olive oil.

2 Anchovy and rosemary

Anchovy fillets	10
Lemon	1
Rosemary leaves	2 tbs
Ex.v.olive oil	4 tbs

Finely chop the anchovies and put into a bowl. Squeeze the lemon juice and finely chop the rosemary.

Mix the lemon juice into the anchovies to 'melt' them, then stir in the rosemary and season with black pepper. Add the olive oil and mix well.

3 Horseradish

Fresh horseradish	100g
White wine vinegar	1 tbs
Lemon	1/2
Crème fraîche	250ml

Peel and grate the horseradish on the fine part of a cheese grater. Add the vinegar and lemon juice, season and stir in the crème fraîche.

4 Salsa verde

Parsley leaves	2 tbs
Mint leaves	1 tbs
Basil leaves	1 tbs
Ex.v.olive oil	
Garlic clove	1
Capers	1 tbs
Anchovy fillets	3
Dijon mustard	1 tsp
Red wine vinegar	1 tbs

Finely chop the parsley, mint and basil, put into a bowl and cover with olive oil. Peel the garlic and chop with the capers and anchovy. Add to the herbs and mix together. Stir in the mustard and vinegar, season with black pepper and add more olive oil to loosen the sauce.

5   Aïoli

Ciabatta loaf	¼
Garlic cloves	3
Egg yolk, organic	1
Ex.v.olive oil	180ml
Lemon	½

Remove the crust from the bread and wet the bread with water. Squeeze out most of the water. Using a pestle and mortar pound the bread with the peeled garlic and 1 tsp salt to a smooth paste. Mix in the egg yolk and then the olive oil drop by drop until you have a thick sauce. Squeeze in the lemon juice and season with black pepper.

6   Salsa rossa piccante

Breadcrumbs	3 tbs
Tomatoes	3
Fresh chillies	4
Dried oregano	1 tbs
Red wine vinegar	1 tbs
Ex.v.olive oil	

Prepare the breadcrumbs (see page 260).

Skin the tomatoes (see page 260). Cut in half, squeeze out the seeds and chop to a pulp. Cut the chillies in half lengthways, scrape out the seeds and finely chop. Mix the tomato pulp with the chilli then stir in the oregano. Add the breadcrumbs and season. Mix in the vinegar and then add enough olive oil to make a thick sauce.

7   Quick tomato

Garlic cloves	3
Basil leaves	1 tbs
Ex.v.olive oil	2 tbs
Tins tomatoes	2 x 400g

Peel and slice the garlic. Heat the olive oil in a thick-bottomed pan and fry the garlic until brown. Add the tomatoes and season. Cook over a high heat, stirring for 15 minutes to break up the tomatoes as they cook preventing them from sticking. Add the basil, olive oil and season.

8 Coarse breadcrumbs

Ciabatta or sourdough loaf

Cut the crusts from the stale bread and discard. Tear the bread into small pieces and pulse-chop in the food processor.

If your bread is fresh, place in a 200°C/Gas 6 oven for 10 minutes until it is crisp but not brown. Let cool then pulse-chop in the food processor.

9 Peeling tomatoes

Use a small sharp knife and make a cut from the stem down the side of each tomato. Put in a bowl and cover with boiling water. After 1/2 minute remove with a slotted spoon into a bowl of cold water. Peel as soon as they are cool enough to touch.

10 Salted anchovies

Rinse each anchovy under a slow-running cold tap to remove any salt crusted to the skin, then carefully pull each fillet off the bone. Discard the head and pull off the fins and tail. Pat dry and use immediately. If using later, squeeze a little lemon juice over and cover with olive oil. They will keep like this for 2 or 3 days.

11 Dried chickpeas

Chickpeas	250g
Bicarbonate of soda	2 tsp
Plain flour	2 tbs
Garlic cloves	2
Fresh chillies	2
Celery stalks	2
Ex.v.olive oil	

Soak the chickpeas overnight in cold water with 1 tsp bicarbonate of soda and 1 tbs plain flour. Peel the garlic. Drain the chickpeas, rinse well and put in a pan with the remaining bicarbonate and plain flour. Cover with cold water. Add the garlic, chillies and celery stalks, and stir.

Bring to the boil and skim off the foam that rises to the surface. Turn the heat down and simmer. After $1/2$ hour add 3 tbs olive oil and 1 tsp sea salt. Continue simmering until the chickpeas are tender. Total cooking time should be no more than $3/4$ hour. Allow them to cool with the vegetables in their liquid.

12 Borlotti and cannellini

Beans	250g
Bicarbonate of soda	2 tbs
Garlic bulb	1
Tomato	1
Sage leaves	3 tsp
Ex.v.olive oil	2 tbs

Soak the beans overnight in cold water with the bicarbonate of soda.

Cut the garlic bulb in half (don't peel). Drain the beans, rinse well and put in a saucepan with the tomato, sage and garlic. Cover with cold water, bring to the boil, removing the froth from the surface. Then reduce the heat, add the olive oil and simmer for 30-45 minutes. When the beans are very tender, remove from heat and let cool in the liquid. Season.

Italian store cupboard

This is a basic list of store cupboard items that you will find useful when using River Cafe Cook Book Easy. Included are items that keep in the cupboard for up to six months and also everyday fresh ingredients to stock up on once a week and keep in the fridge.

We suggest always keeping tinned tomatoes, and for quick soups good quality tinned cannellini and borlotti beans. Essentials to keep in the bottom of the fridge are red onions, celery, garlic, and a few fresh herbs such as flat-leaf parsley and basil in season.

Choose an olive oil for cooking, and an extra virgin single estate oil for bruschettas, soups, and drizzling.

Cupboard

sea salt
black peppercorns
dried red chillies
bay leaves (fresh or dried)
dried oregano
fennel seeds
nutmeg
stock cubes

capers
anchovies
black olives
extra virgin olive oil
red wine vinegar
aged balsamic vinegar
white wine
red wine
dijon mustard

tinned tomatoes
cannellini beans
borlotti beans
chickpeas
dried porcini
lentils (Puy or Casteluccio)

plain flour
semolina flour
risotto rice
polenta
spaghetti
tagliatelle
short pasta

70% chocolate
blanched whole almonds

Fridge

unsalted butter
creme fraiche
parmesan cheese
free range organic eggs
pancetta

garlic
red onions
celery
flat-leaf parsley
sage
basil
thyme
marjoram

Suppliers

Cambridge
Cambridge Cheese Company
All Saints Passage
Cambridge CB2 3LS
01223 328 672

Cheltenham
The Fine Cheese Company Ltd
5 Regent Street
Cheltenham GL50 1HE
01242 255 022
(Italian provisions)

Dorset
Trenchermans
The Old Dairy
Crompton Park
Sherbourne
Dorset DT9 4QO
Fax: 01935 432 857

East Sussex
Beckworth's Deli
67 High Street
Lewes
East Sussex BN7 1XG
01273 474 502

Greater Manchester
Chorlton Wholefoods
34 Beech Road
Chorlton-Cum-Hardy
M21 1EL

Herefordshire
Ceci Paulo
21 High Street
Ledbury
Herefordshire HR8 1DS
01531 632 976
(Italian provisions)

Lancashire
Ramsbottom Victuallers
16-18 Market Place
Ramsbottom
01706 825 070

Leeds
Beano Wholefoods
Workers Co-op
36 New Briggate
Leeds LS1 6NV
0113 243 5737
www.beanowholefoods.co.uk

Harvey Nichols Food Market
107-111 Briggate
Victoria Quarter
Leeds LS1 6AZ

Leicester
Stones Deli
2-6 St Martins Walk
St Martins Square
Leicester LE1 5DG
0116 261 4430

Liverpool
No 7 Delicatessen
15 Faulkner Street
Liverpool
0151 709 9633

London
Allens
117 Mount Street
London W1K 3LA
020 7499 5831
www.allensofmayfair.co.uk
(Meat & game)

Baker and Spice
75 Salusbury Road
London NW6 6NH
020 7604 3636
41 Denyer Street
London SW3 2LX
020 7589 4736
www.bakerandspice.com
(Sourdough bread)

Blagdens Fishmongers
65 Paddington Street
London W1U 4JQ
020 7935 8321
blagfish@vossnet.co.uk
(Fish, game, poultry)

Brindisa
32 Exmouth Market
London EC1 4QE
020 7713 1666
(Dried beans, salted anchovies)

Clarke's
24 Kensington Church Street
London W8 4BH
020 7221 9225
www.clarkes.co.uk
(Breads, cheese, River Cafe olive oil)

The Conran Shop
81 Fulham Road
London SW3 6RD
020 7723 2223
55 Marylebone High Street
London W1 5HS
020 7589 7401
(River Cafe olive oil)

The Fish Shop at
Kensington Place
201 Kensington Church Street
London W8 7LX
020 7243 6626
(Fish, olive oil, vinegar, a
selection of unusual vegetables)

Frank Godfry Butchers
7 Highbury Park
London N5 1QJ
020 7226 2425

Fresh and Wild
210 Westbourne Grove
London W11 2RH
020 7229 1063
www.freshandwild.com
(Organic vegetables, pulses,
tinned vegetables, Green &
Black's chocolate)

Jeroboams
96 Holland Park Avenue
London W11 3AA
020 7727 9359
www.jeroboams.co.uk
beth.jeans@jeroboams.co.uk
(Italian cheese, sourdough bread)

La Fromagerie
30 Highbury Park
London N5 2SS
020 7359 7440
2-4 Moxon Street
London W1 4EW
020 7935 0341
(Italian cheese, Italian
vegetables, Pugliese bread)

La Maree
76 Sloane Avenue
London SW3 3D2
020 7589 8067
(Fish)

Lidgate Butchers
110 Holland Park Avenue
London W11 4UA
020 7727 8243

Lina Stores
18 Brewer Street
London W1R 3FS
020 7437 6482
(Italian provisions)

Luigi's
349 Fulham Road
London SW10 9TW
020 7352 7739
(Italian provisions)

Macken and Collins
35 Turnham Green Terrace
London W4 1RG
020 8995 0140
www.m/and/c.co.uk
(Italian vegetables, puntarelles)

Maison Blanc
Branches throughout UK – check
web.
www.maisonblanc.co.uk
(Sourdough bread, country
loaves, French loaves)

Maquis Shop
111 Hammersmith Grove
London W6 0NG
020 8846 3850
(Bread & Italian provisions,
barbeques)

Michanicou Bros
2 Clarendon Road
London W11 3AA
020 7727 5191
(Italian vegetables)

Montes Delicatessen
23a Canonbury Lane
London N1 2AS
020 7354 4335
(River Cafe olive oil, Italian
vegetables)

Mortimer and Bennett
33 Turnham Green Terrace
London W4 1RG
020 8995 4145
www.mortimerandbennett.com
(Italian provisions)

Neal's Yard Dairy
17 Shorts Garden
London WC2H 9AT
020 7645 3532
(Cheese, crème fraiche)

Panzer's
13-19 Circus Road
London NW8 5PB
020 7722 8596
www.panzers.co.uk
(Italian vegetables)

Planet Organic
42 Westbourne Grove
London W2 55H
020 7221 7171

Poilane
42-46 Elizabeth Street
London SW1W 9PA
020 7808 4910
www.poilane.fr
(Sourdough bread)

Randalls Butchers
113 Wandsworth Bridge Road
London SW6 2TE
020 7386 3426
(Organic meat and poultry)

The River Cafe
Thames Wharf
Rainville Road
London W6 9HA
020 7386 4200
www.rivercafe.co.uk
(River Cafe olive oil)

Rococo
321 King's Road
London SW3 5EP
020 7352 5857
www.rococochocolates.com
(Chocolate)

The Salusbury
56 Salusbury Road
London NW6 6NN
020 7328 3287
(Italian provisions & vegetables)

Tavola
155 Westbourne Grove
London W11 2RS
020 7229 0571
(Italian provisions)

Vallebona
Unit 14, 59 Weir Street
London SW19 8UG
020 8944 5665
www.vallebona.co.uk
info@vallebona.co.uk
(Mail order, Italian specialities)

Villandry
170 Great Portland Street
London W1N 5TB
020 7631 3131
www.villandry.com
(Italian vegetables, bread,
chocolate)

Manchester

Save The Day
345 Deansgate
Manchester M3
0161 834 2266
1 The Dome
The Trafford Centre
Manchester M17 8DA
0161 629 1234

North Yorkshire

Archimboldo's
146 King's Road
Harrogate
North Yorkshire HG1 5HY
01423 508 760

Oxfordshire

Abingdon
Wells Stores
Peachcroft Farm
Abingdon OX14 2HP
01235 535 978

Shrewsbury

Appleyards Deli
85 Wyle Cop
Shrewsbury SY1 1VT
01743 240 180

Somerset

The Olive Garden Deli
87 Hill Road
Cleveden
North Somerset B521 7TN
01275 341 222

Southampton

Sunnyfields Organic Farm
Jacobs Gutter Lane
Totton
Southampton SO40 9FX
0118 984 2392
(Cavolo nero, Swiss chard, many
varieties of beetroot and squash)

Surrey

Secretts Farm Shop
Hurst Farm
Chapel Lane
Milford
Godalming
Surrey GU8 5HU
01483 520 540
(Italian provisions)

Yorkshire

Heber Wines
34 Swadford Street
Skipton
North Yorkshire BD23 1RD
01756 795 815

Ireland

Belfast

Feasts
39 Dublin Road
Belfast
Northern Ireland BT2 7HD
02890 332 787
(Italian provisions)

Dublin

Denis Healy
Templebar Market
Saturday 9.30-5.30
00 353 872 485 826

Scotland

Edinburgh

Valvona and Crolla Ltd
19 Elm Row
Edinburgh EH7 4AA
0131 556 6066
www.valvonacrolla.com
(Olive oil, Italian provisions,
bottarga, sourdough bread,
Italian vegetables)

Glasgow

Grass Roots
Woodlands Road
0141 353 3278
(Italian provisions)

Hearts Buchanan
Byres Road
0141 334 7626
(Italian provisions)

Wales

Hay Wholefoods & Deli
Lion Street
Hay-on-Wye
Herefordshire HR3 5AA
01497 820 708
patriciahharrison@cecipaolo.com

Italy

Ai due Catini d'Oro sas
di Zecchin Rino e Co
Piazza dei Frutti, 46
35122 Padova
00 39 49 8750623
(Mustard essence)

Farmers' Markets

Borough Market
8 Southwark Street
Pool of London
London SE1 1TL
020 7407 1002
Open Friday and Saturday
www.boroughmarket.org.uk
info@boroughmarket.org.uk

General Farmers Markets
www.farmersmarkets.org.uk

London Farmers' Market
www.lfm.org.uk
020 7359 1936

Mail Order

Espero
www.espero.it
(Italian provisions)

The Portobello Food
Company Ltd
020 8748 0505
www.portobellofoods.com
London-based same-day delivery
(Italian provisions, Italian
vegetables)

Index

The authors would like to thank: Editor **Lesley McOwan** Recipe Editor **Susan Fleming** Designer **David Eldridge** Artworker **Marisa Sebastian** Editorial Assistants **Sue Birtwistle, Lucy Boyd, Jan Dalley, Ian Heide** Additional Photographers **Jeremy Hudson, Gary Calton,** Chefs **Theo Randall, April Bloomfield, Sian Wyn-Owen, Matthew Armistead, Joanne Wilkinson, Joseph Trivelli, Stephen Beadle, Felicity Southwell, Theodore Hill, Jan Gillies, Helio Fenerich All staff past and present at the River Cafe** & **Vashti Armit, Ossie Gray, Lynsey Hird, Charles Pullan, Ed Victor,** Richard Rogers, and David MacIlwaine.

River Cafe Books

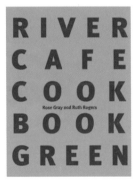

First published in 2003   9 10 8   Text copyright © Rose Gray and Ruth Rogers 2003. Photographs copyright © Martyn Thompson. Bruschetta photographs numbers 1, 5, 9, 13, 16, 19, 20 and 21 on pages 10 to 15; 33; 188 and 189 copyright © Jeremy Hudson. Photograph on page 6 copyright © Gary Calton. Frozen Sculpture copyright © Marc Quinn. Rose Gray and Ruth Rogers have asserted their right to be identified as authors of this work in accordance with the Copyright, Design and Patents Act 1988. All rights reserved. No part of this publication may be reproduced, stored in a retrieval system, or transmitted in any form or by any means, electronic, mechanical, photocopying, recording or otherwise, without the prior permission of the copyright owners. First published in the United Kingdom in 2003 by Ebury Press, Random House, 20 Vauxhall Bridge Road, London SW1V 2SA; Random House Australia (Pty) Limited, 20 Alfred Street, Milsons Point, Sydney, New South Wales 2061, Australia; Random House New Zealand Limited, 18 Poland Road, Glenfield, Auckland 10, New Zealand; Random House (Pty) Limited, Endulini, 5A Jubilee Road, Parktown 2193, South Africa. Random House UK Limited Reg. No. 954009, www.randomhouse.co.uk. Papers used by Ebury Press are natural, recyclable products made from wood grown in sustainable forests. A CIP catalogue record is available for this book from the British Library. ISBN 0091884640.